Education, Psychoanalysis, and Social Transformation

Series Editors:
jan jagodzinski, University of Alberta
Mark Bracher, Kent State University

The purpose of this series is to develop and disseminate psychoanalytic and psychotherapeutic knowledge—including knowledge derived from cognitive science, neuroscience, new emotion studies, and other emerging fields—that can help educators in their pursuit of three core functions of education:

1. facilitating student learning,
2. fostering students' personal development, and
3. promoting prosocial attitudes, habits, and behaviors in students (i.e., those opposed to poverty, inequality, ethnocentrism, nationalism, racism, sexism, heterosexism, violence, substance abuse, etc.).

Psychoanalytic knowledge can help educators realize these aims of education by providing crucial understanding of:

1. the emotional and cognitive capabilities that are necessary for students to be able to learn, to develop, and to engage in prosocial behavior,
2. the motivations that drive such learning, development, and behaviors,
3. the motivations that produce antisocial behaviors as well as resistance to learning and development, and
4. the principles, techniques, and practices of intervention that promote the development of optimal emotional and cognitive capabilities.

Such understanding can enable educators to develop pedagogical strategies, techniques, and practices to help students overcome psychological impediments to learning and development as well as to the adequate and fair assessment of other individuals and groups. By offering an understanding of the motivations and the emotional and cognitive deficiencies that cause some of our most severe social problems—including poverty, inequality, crime, violence, substance abuse, and prejudice—together with knowledge of the types of interventions through which these psychological impediments can be corrected, books in this series will contribute to the reduction and prevention of such problems, a task that education is increasingly being called upon to assume.

Radical Pedagogy: Identity, Generativity, and Social Transformation
By Mark Bracher

Teaching the Rhetoric of Resistance: The Popular Holocaust and Social Change in a Post 9/11 World
By Robert Samuels

Television and Youth Culture: Televised Paranoia
By jan jagodzinski

Psychopedagogy: Freud, Lacan, and the Psychoanalytic Theory of Education
By K. Daniel Cho

New Media, Cultural Studies, and Critical Theory after Postmodernism: Automodernity from Zizek to Lacalu
By Robert Samuels

Visual Art and Education in an Era of Designer Capitalism: Deconstructing the Oral Eye
By jan jagodzinski

A Deleuzian Approach to Curriculum: Essays on a Pedagogical Life
By Jason J. Wallin

A Therapeutic Approach to Teaching Poetry: Individual Development, Psychology, and Social Reparation
By Todd O. Williams

Resistance to Learning: Overcoming the Desire Not to Know in Classroom Teaching
By Marshall Wise Alcorn Jr.

Resistance to Learning
Overcoming the Desire Not to Know in Classroom Teaching

Marshall Wise Alcorn Jr.

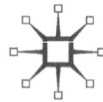

RESISTANCE TO LEARNING
Copyright © Marshall Wise Alcorn Jr., 2013.
Softcover reprint of the hardcover 1st edition 2013 978-1-137-00285-3

All rights reserved.

First published in 2013 by
PALGRAVE MACMILLAN®
in the United States—a division of St. Martin's Press LLC,
175 Fifth Avenue, New York, NY 10010.

Where this book is distributed in the UK, Europe and the rest of the world, this is by Palgrave Macmillan, a division of Macmillan Publishers Limited, registered in England, company number 785998, of Houndmills, Basingstoke, Hampshire RG21 6XS.

Palgrave Macmillan is the global academic imprint of the above companies and has companies and representatives throughout the world.

Palgrave® and Macmillan® are registered trademarks in the United States, the United Kingdom, Europe and other countries.
ISBN 978-1-349-43397-1   ISBN 978-1-137-31856-5 (eBook)
DOI 10.1057/9781137318565

Library of Congress Cataloging-in-Publication Data

Alcorn, Marshall W., 1949–
   Resistance to Learning : overcoming the desire not to know in classroom teaching / Marshall Alcorn.
      pages cm.—(Education, psychoanalysis, and social transformation)
   Includes bibliographical references and index.
   ISBN 978–1–137–00285–3 (hardback)
   1. Educational psychology. 2. Education, Higher. I. Title.
LB1051.A3725 2013
370.15—dc23   2013011570

A catalogue record of the book is available from the British Library.

Design by Newgen Knowledge Works (P) Ltd., Chennai, India.

First edition: September 2013

10 9 8 7 6 5 4 3 2 1

To the next generation: Jewell and Jasmine Alcorn,
Austin and Tyler Alcorn, Skye and Sean Alcorn

Contents

Preface: On Gaps, Pauses, and Silences in Coming to Know   ix
Acknowledgments   xi

One	The Emotional Demands of Information Assimilation	1
Two	The Psychology and Biology of the Desire Not to Know	43
Three	Symptomatic Fixation, Emotion, and Social Alliance	93
Four	Academic Allegiance and Attacks on Linking	125
Five	Information Relays and the Touched Nerves of Global Injustice	153

Bibliography   179
Index   187

Preface: On Gaps, Pauses, and Silences in Coming to Know

> *"There are poetic reversals like this in life, is my point. There are pauses between knowing and understanding. Pauses in which we wait for delayed news about ourselves to spark along the sagging wires."*
> —Amity Gaige, *Schroder*

Amity Gaige's novel features a character, Schroder, who is interested in the various words that demarcate gaps between ongoing links of thought. Periods, for example, mark the end of a sentence where a reader digests what has been said and prepares for a new sentence. In particular instances of speech, one can notice a longer gap between sentences. Here, in this longer gap, we may describe our recognition of a pause. Pauses reveal a certain slowness in the digestive process of thought. Pauses are not gaps marked by periods but by temporal delays in the mind's assimilation of thought. Pauses, though they are empty spaces, may in fact be meaningful in and of themselves. Pauses introduce the idea that something additional is going on between two linked sentences. Something more is present to a thinking mind than the verbal representation of the sentences might suggest. In addition to pauses, there are gaps still longer and more potent. A long pause becomes at some point registered as a "silence." When we notice silence, it often speaks volumes. Silence can be "telling," but it can also be invisible.

This book is an attempt to make visible what is often invisible in those "pauses in which we wait for delayed news about ourselves to spark along the sagging wires" (Gaige, 125). Between "knowing and understanding" are complex and usually invisible processes of mind that allow "knowing" to become marked as "understanding." This book is about something I have termed "the emotional assimilation of thought," and its opposite "the desire not to know." I am not happy with the terms I have chosen, but I am seeking a language to slow down and observe what may not be seen.

Some sentences and their busy ideas connect quickly and easily. It can be a joy to read lively prose, with its rich implication of more enjoyment to come. Some words, however, make us pause. They require "emotional work." Some sentences stop us in our tracks. The emotional work of these thoughts may seem unbearable. This book is an attempt to honor and give respect to these last two categories.

The pause between knowing and understanding may be small, almost imperceptible in recognition. And yet often everything depends on this link—a link that may well fail rather than succeed. Michelle Masse has recently argued that teachers must learn to work "within the suspended liminal time of knowing/not knowing" (Masse, 2011) This book offers approximately 200 pages of commentary that seeks to understand and more carefully attend to this suspended liminal time, a time of pauses, silences, and reverie.

Acknowledgments

This book reflects the influence of many people in many places over many years. I want to express my heartfelt thanks to those close to memory, whose thinking has become interwoven with my own. In large measure the book is the result of almost 20 years of spirited engagement with the Association for the Psychoanalysis of Culture and Society. My good friend Mark Bracher and I cofounded the organization in 1994 with the late Claudia Tate. In the last 20 years (almost) our group has been renewed by an energetic leadership featuring Marilyn Charles and Michael O'Loughlin, Elizabeth Young-Bruehl, Fred Alford, Robert Samuels, Jean Wyatt, Lynn Layton, Peter Redman, Michelle Masse, Rico Ainslee, Simon Clarke, John Bird, Jan Haaken, Karl Figlio, Esther Rashkin, jan jagodzinski, Todd McGowan, Hilary Neroni, Henry Krips, and Jennifer Freidlander. I am lucky to be able to spend time with so many smart, capable, and dependable people and to have been able to do so over so many years of conferences, meetings, dinners, and emails.

I am also much indebted to participation in the Washington Psychoanalytic Society, first as a research candidate and then later as an active teacher and committee member. I would like to thank my analyst Judith Chused for five years of dedicated work. I would also like to thank my former teachers and now colleagues: Bob Winer, Rick Waugaman, Dick Fritsch, Art Blank, Marc Levine, Don Ross, Doug Chavis, Kathy Burton, Kathy Brunkow, Don Ross, David Cooper, Sharon Alperovitz, Liz Hersh, Karyn Messina, Nydia Lisman-Pieczanski, Lindsay Clarkson, Carla Eliot Neely, Pat Crowe, Tony Hani, David Levi, J. David Miller, Stephen Paly, Scott Twentyman, John Kafka, John Zinner, Ernie Wallwork, Al Leblanc, Cornelia Lischewski, Derek Hawver, and Susan Lazar.

I have spent much time engaged with our Washington, DC Lacan study group, now formalized as the Lacanian Forum of

Washington, DC. Our membership is Wilfried Ver Eecke, Macario Giraldo, Devra Simiu, Brian Casemore, Edmond Degaiffier, Gabriela Zorzutti, Nora Gabbert, Jennifer Braun, and Stephen Whitworth. Our group has been much enriched by generous visits from Collette Soler, Luiz Izcovich, and Sol Aparaicio

I have profited greatly from my Washington Psychoanalytic Institute Book Group. Our membership is Bob Winer, Bo Winer, Rick Waugaman, Elizabeth Waugaman, Art Blank, Alex Smirnov, Mary Jo Pebbles, Chris Keats, Denise Forte, Jim Hutchinson, and Chris Erskine.

My thinking has been enlivened by participation in the Washington Forum on Psychiatry and the Humanities. I would like to particularly thank Gordon Kirschner and the group, Stanley Palumbo, Wilfried Ver Eecke, Macrio Giraldo, and Joe Brent.

I appreciate the continuing support I have received from my department at George Washington University. I would particularly like to thank Jeffrey Cohen, Gil Harris, Tara Wallace, Gayle Wald, Jim Miller, Tony Lopez, Jennifer James, Judy Plotz, Kavita Daiya, Jenny Green-Lewis, Tom Mallon, David McAleavey, Chris Sten, Bob Combs, Bob Ganz, Jane Shore, and Faye Moskowitz in the English department. And friends in other disciplines—Alf Hiltebeitel, Andrew Zimmerman, Brian Casemore, Gail Weiss, and Peter Caws.

In recent years I would like to thank in particular a group of students and professors who have worked with me on the study of trauma and neuroscience—Dmityi Galkin, Patrick Cook, Evelyn Schreiber, Patty Chu, Anton Trinidad, Marilena Zacheos, Jen Cho, Michael O'Neil, James Francis, Amy Baily, Ilya Kavalerov, and Bridget Williams.

The main bulk of this book was written in the mountains of North Carolina in the summer of 2012. I am indebted to my good neighbors there, Jill Holmes and Sally Jacobson, Terry and Cindy Murphy, John and Brenda Czipri for warm homes and good cheer.

As I grow older I increasingly appreciate the accidents of my birth. I have learned and continue to learn from my two brothers, Patrick Alcorn, SAS, and Col. David Alcorn, USAF. Many years of discussion with them have helped me appreciate the thinking of smart people who have worked in endeavors very different from my own. The three of us have taken on unusual tasks. Our meetings always remind us of what we share. I appreciate the learning skills each of us have developed in managing different life tasks. I thank as well my sons, Skye Alcorn and Sean Alcorn, who have contributed significantly to this book with ongoing conversations over the last ten years. I am proud of their achievements and grateful for their company.

I owe particular thanks to people who read earlier, largely unreadable portions of this manuscript. They all offered suggestions and were generous with advice and encouragement. Thank you, Chris Erskine, Mark Bracher, Fred Alford, Jean Wyatt, Patrick Cook, Jim Hansell, and Michelle Masse. I am also greatly indebted to my friends Brian Casemore, Peter Filene, and Mike O'Neil, who read and helped to fine-tune near-final drafts of the chapters. I owe, in addition, special thanks to my friends Terry Rizzuti and Wil Scott, who have helped me understand the particular nature of combat trauma memory, and information assimilation.

Finally I wish to express thanks to my wife, Christine Erskine, who has contributed to and enlivened (for me anyway) this project in countless ways. Shared intellectual projects are much happier than solitary ones.

Washington, DC
March 1, 2013

Chapter One
The Emotional Demands of Information Assimilation

American literary critic and rhetorician Stanley Fish has argued that people are not significantly moved by the use of evidence in reasoning. A dramatic example is Fish's denial of the usefulness of evidence in proving the historical validity of the Holocaust. In a review of the April 2000 London court case between eminent Emory historian Deborah Lipstadt and "Holocaust denier" David Irving, Fish argued that it was incorrect of Lipstadt to "rest her case" upon an apparent distinction between "irrefutable evidence" and "myth, rationality, and bigotry" (Fish 2001, 500). Lipstadt was sued by Irving because she claimed that he had distorted historical evidence. Fish does not deny that Irving and his group belong to the "radical right and the lunatic left." He does deny that something like "irrefutable evidence" can exist and have force to influence thought.

For Fish, thought, in essence, is not an act of reason, but a repetition of belief. Evidence cannot change thought, because thought always begins repetitively as an interpretive bias toward evidence. "True belief does not emerge from reason's chain; rather true belief—and false belief too—configure reason's chain and determine in advance what will be seen as reasonable and what will be recognized as evidence" (Fish 2001, 501).

Gary Olson and Lynn Worsham represent Fish's argument by asserting that for Fish it is not the case that "seeing is believing." Instead the relation between evidence and reasoning works in reverse. We do not observe the world and then believe what we see. We have beliefs and we then observe or hallucinate the truth of our beliefs in our observation of the world. In this case "believing is seeing" (Olson and Worsham 2004, 149). We invest the world with properties it does not have in order to confirm our beliefs. The world may be full of information, but most people ignore or dismiss whatever they find uncomfortable to think about. A strong reading of Fish would suggest that humans routinely falsify evidence through hallucination.

Fish's claims about evidence, reason, and the possibilities of education have been widely attacked, but also reluctantly acknowledged. An uncomfortably strong argument supporting Fish's claims regarding hallucinatory evidence can now be made by way of medical research. New tools for examining the brain's structure and biology offer us a picture of it being slow to recognize and accommodate new information. Information taken into memory may be stored in various areas of the brain without being made available to problem-solving centers. In this book I will I call this problem a "desire not to know." I will examine concrete examples that illustrate the truth of Fish's claim about evidence. My general argument, however, has two parts. First, I will give careful attention to how particular minds resist evidence. Second, I will suggest that failures in the use of evidence are not as hopeless as Fish contends. People can indeed be brought made to abandon hallucinations and make use of "irrefutable facts." This integration of evidence, however, is not through the work of reason, but through the "work" of emotion. This book will shift between neurological accounts of the mind and close observations of particular minds in order to support a case for the primacy of emotion in the development of an educated mind. My emphasis will be upon classroom teaching in the liberal arts and the role emotion plays in the processing of thought.

I begin my discussion with a remarkable set of experiments developed by V. S. Ramachandran, director of the Center for Brain and Cognition at the University of California, San Diego. Ramachandran has made major contributions to the study of phantom limb phenomenon, visual processes, and cognitive function. Trained as a medical doctor, he became interested in a medical condition termed anosognosia in which an individual is unable to recognize that a part of their body is paralyzed. Anosognosia, he writes, "is an extraordinary syndrome about which almost nothing is known. The patient is obviously sane in most respects yet claims to see her lifeless limb springing into action" (Ramachandran 1999, 131). Ramachandran's patients, like the true believers of Fish's discourse communities, can make no use of "irrefutable information." Fish does not explain why this apparently psychotic behavior exists; Ramachandran does. Fish does not believe this apparently psychotic behavior can be remedied. Ramachandran demonstrates how it can.

In the chapters that follow I will pursue a very traditional theme, the problem of human rationality, but I hope to address this problem from a very new perspective. Like many I do not believe that rationality can be systematically defined. There are many different kinds of rationality for many different kinds of discourses and human communities. In this book, rationality is meaningful only in terms of a simple criterion. Can a mind, seeking to solve a problem, make use of information perceived as relevant to that problem? Patients suffering from anosognosia will, Ramachandran shows, reach out to grasp a tray with a glass of water, assume that both arms work, and watch perplexed as the tray and glass fall on the floor.

This book will show many examples of minds responding to pertinent information by first "witnessing" and then subsequently "forgetting" information. These minds (even the anosognosia patients, I will show) first take a step to "recognize" information, and then take a second step to "contain" this information, and yet in the next step of thought, these same minds—owing to fear, anxiety, or dissociation—will forget, dismiss, or deny the information that was initially accepted. This step-by-step response to possibilities for problem solving is described by Fish as "chains of reason" and by clinical literature as the "linking" of thought representations. My intent is not to police or enforce some particular definition of rationality, but rather to observe and understand how minds fail to develop linked thoughts they themselves initiate to solve problems.

Since Plato the Western world has represented the mind as a spacious interiority capable of infinitely subtle and flexible formulations of rational thought and imagination. This heroic mind is the subject of Plato's *Phaedrus* and has been the human mind imagined by science since the dawn of the Enlightenment. This naturally empowered rational mind has the capacity to take human progress to unimagined ends and is impaired only by the polluting presence of emotion and passion.

A different understanding of the human mind is now emerging. Ramachandran's work, along with many other research studies in many fields, supports Stanley Fish's claim that "believing is seeing." People will invent evidence to support belief before they will adjust belief in response to evidence. Ramachandran describes how patients with anosognosia will "see" their paralyzed arms perform multiple and complex actions while these same arms are in fact lying lifeless at their sides. And they will maintain these claims even when the doctor is present to point to a useless limb and argue with their own improbable observations. These patients seem sane in every respect, but they apparently hallucinate the use of immobile arms. Ramachandran argues, surprisingly, that these patients are representative of the human capacity for denial.

There are two qualities in this narrative of hallucinating anosognosia patients that are particularly noteworthy for teachers. First, these people seem sane in every respect. You could talk to these people about many things, find them logical and thoughtful, and never suspect that in relation to one issue, one that is very important to their lives, they literally cannot see the hand in front of their nose. In respect to this one truth claim, they are utterly incapable of not only "reason" but also reporting the truth of perception itself. Second, within this one very restricted field of vision that helps define, if not their belief system, at least their sense of emotional security, they will rely upon and defend the most unimaginable and "psychotic" verbal assertions with a fluent production of "thought" and ideation that they themselves seem to experience as absolutely persuasive.

Ramachandran was intrigued with these patients because he could not initially really believe what he saw. When Stanley Fish describes the beliefs of Holocaust deniers, or "true believers," we do not get a careful representation of a particular mind involved in an act of thinking. This failure of focus impedes our understanding. Ramachandran's work offers a more accurate account of Fish's most unsettling ideas. Minds do refute facts, but the ground of such refutation, while emotional, is also responsive to developmental integration.

Ramachandran's interest in the "unthinkable" denials of the clearly "irrefutable evidence" of paralysis led him to pursue a number of experiments. He sought to grasp the basic principles of the response. Is such denial biological or psychological? On the one hand, there was evidence to support the idea that the condition was the result of purely biological malfunctions in the brain. And yet, on the other hand, he found that these apparently "biological" instances of denial could be remedied by "psychological" procedures that did not repair any biological malfunction.

Over time Ramachandran came to feel that his work with these patients represented the universal drama of human denial: "Watching these patients is like observing human nature through a magnifying lens: I'm reminded of all aspects of human folly and of how prone to self-deception we all are" (Ramachandran 1999, 130). If Ramachandran is right that "we"—students and teachers—exhibit these seemingly crazy instances of denial, what does this mean for education? What does it mean for democracy? Should teachers think differently about students "resistant" to fact and reason? These are the themes this book will explore.

Everyday Unimaginable Stupidity

I have come to believe that the denial we see in Ramachandran's anosognosia patients represents a huge, but generally dismissed dimension of everyday social life. We could call this practice "everyday unimaginable stupidity." This is stupidity on such an enormous scale that those of us who observe it are not fully able to comprehend it. We see it, and then, because it defeats our ability to make sense of it, cannot contain it. In the realm of law, medicine, education, politics, and personal relations, crucial information is routinely denied, forgotten, or dismissed. This fact by itself is disturbing, but even more disturbing is our general tendency to not recognize the consequences and the implications of the denials that take place.

If one is attentive to the kind of "thinking" formulated by patients with anosognosia, one soon begins to question the essential nature of what we think of as "the mind." In one particular example a woman with a paralyzed arm denies that the arm that is attached to her body is her own arm. The doctor grasps the woman's lifeless left arm and holds it in front of her eyes. "Whose arm is this?" he asks the woman. She claims it is her brother's arm.

What we observe in this encounter is an extended dialogic engagement with a "mind" that does not perform the way we expect it to. On the one hand, this mind is fully present to talk to the doctor. There is nothing to indicate anything mentally "wrong" with the speaker. On the other hand, this mind's ability to observe the world and talk about what it sees is severely compromised. At key points in the flow of "thought" the patient has no apparent awareness of logical language or simple rules of perception. What is this mind doing?

There are, of course, a number of purely rational problems associated with the patient claiming that the arm attached to her shoulder belongs to her brother. First, we are told that her brother lives in Texas and she is in a hospital in Oxford, England. Second, this arm is attached to her own body.

A mind should be responsive to the clear and "irrefutable evidence" of sense logic, and verbal continuity. A mind should take responsibility for this evidence: If you are carrying an arm attached to your shoulder, it is logically your own arm. Such apparently abstract and ineffectual rational claims, however, have no influence on the patient's thought. Whatever evidence the doctor formulates to convince her that her arm is her own, she dismisses easily. This evidence has no effect on the confidence of her reasoning. Ramachandran asks her how she knows it is her brother's arm. She has a completely convincing answer: "Because it is big and hairy."

Ramachandran observes: "To listen to a patient deny ownership of her arm and yet, in the same breath, admit that it is attached to her shoulder is one of the most perplexing phenomenona that one can encounter as a neurologist" (1999, 132–133).

Such denial is indeed perplexing, but it is not so uncommon. Similar (though not quite so dramatic) examples of outright denial of observed "real world" evidence occur frequently. Psychologist Daniel Goleman argues that we deflect psychological pain by keeping uncomfortable thoughts out of our minds. "The brain's basic design," he argues, "offers a prototype of how we handle pain of all sorts, including psychological distress and social anxieties" (Goleman 1985, 29).

Some examples of information repudiation, however, seem difficult to explain in terms of the threat of pain. In the 1980s two researchers tested how well students in a first year college physics course learned basic concepts (Halloun and Hestenes 1985). They postulated that "common sense" understandings of motion were very different from Newtonian understandings of motion; and they wanted to see how well introductory courses in college physics changed these students' common sense understandings. What they found was that students often do not learn what they are taught—even when they pass tests that demonstrate that they have learned it. Not only did students not change how they thought as the result of a course they spent a semester thinking about and passing, but they also did not change how they thought even when immediate evidence logically required a change. When they were called in to witness a physics experiment demonstrating the falsehood of their beliefs, they continued to insist upon the validity of their false beliefs. Ken Bain, a scholar of education, summarizes their findings thus:

> The students performed all kinds of mental gymnastics to avoid confronting and revising the fundamental underlying principles that guided their understanding... some of these students had received high grades in the class. (2004, 23)

In this example we do not see people failing to observe the shared physical world. We do see minds observe the world, consider this "evidence," and yet in a third act of thought, dismiss the observed evidence.

Like Ramachandran investigating the mind of the anosognosia patient, these researchers observed the minds of everyday students. Ken Bain, who reports on this experiment, describes the reaction of the researchers to their experiment: "What they observed astonished them" (2004, 23). Students observed clear physical experiments that disproved their ideas about motion; nonetheless, they refused to change their initial beliefs

Bain and Ramachandran offer us glimpses into a world of the inner workings of thought that is both all too common and generally neglected. If we begin to look, these examples of the mind not taking in evidence are everywhere. Some of these events are relatively harmless and even humorous. Bill Bryson, writing about his hike along the Appalachian Trail, records his conversation with another hiker about a tent. This woman looks at his tent and comments: "You should have got a three season tent." He responds: "It is a three season tent." The conversation continues:

> "Pardon me saying so, but it is like seriously dumb to come out here in March without a three season tent."
> "It is a three season tent."
> "You're lucky you haven't frozen yet..."

> "Believe me it is a three season tent."
> "That's a three season tent." (The woman points to another tent.)
> "That's exactly the same tent."
> She glanced at it again. "Whatever. How many miles did you do today?" (Bryson 1998, 74)

Bryson's dialogue is something we might recognize as familiar. A conversation between two people begins with a simple factual observation. One person makes a simple factual claim and the other person attempts to correct the facts of the claim. The conversation should be able to explore the various kinds of evidence in support of the differing truth claims. Instead the conversation becomes only a series of assertions without any thoughtful attempt to focus on a claim and evaluate evidence.

In this example, there are repeated attempts to prompt another person to consider—at least as a provisional thought—relatively simple information. The information introduced is repeatedly dismissed. At the point where evidence is convincing, the person who introduced the topic changes the subject as if no previous conversation existed. In this example, the apparent obstinate failure to take in information is funny. But failures of information are not always funny. Failures to take in information occur in corporate boardrooms, in university classes, in personal relations, and in political decision making. They are everyday occurrences, they are everywhere, and often they are catastrophic.

Rick Shenkman, historian and author of *Just How Stupid Are We? Facing the Truth about the American Voter*, points out in a September 7, 2008, article in the *Washington Post*:

> Just before the 2003 invasion of Iraq, after months of unsubtle hinting from Bush administration officials, some 60 percent of Americans had come to believe that Iraq was behind the Sept. 11, 2001, terrorist attacks, despite the absence of evidence for the claim, according to a series of surveys taken by the PIPA/Knowledge Networks poll. A year later, after the bipartisan, independent 9/11 Commission reported that Saddam Hussein had had nothing to do with al-Qaeda's assaults on the World Trade Center and the Pentagon, 50 percent of Americans still insisted that he did. In other words, the public was bluntly given the data by a group of officials generally believed to be credible—and it still didn't absorb the most basic facts about the most important event of their time.

These are everyday facts; their failures of recognition have costly effects in terms of financial expense and loss of life. These events are the political equivalents of Hurricane Katrina and the Gulf War. And yet their occurrence is only briefly noticed. Their disastrous consequences become almost invisible.

Resistance to new information is both ubiquitous and largely untheorized.[1] Research in political science indicates that many people with bias do not correct their ideas when given creditable information. Bain's work on education proposes that much teaching routinely fails to deliver the cognitive change that is its purpose. I will cite examples from medicine, law, politics, and education to suggest that evidence is routinely dismissed, precisely at a point where it is needed. Increasingly politicians stage debates in which the truth of the various claims is essentially irrelevant. There have been many appeals that we must work harder to make this truth available to people. I suggest that we should not invest great hope in the effectiveness of simply making "truth" available. We must present evidence, but we must equally seek to understand how and in what conditions people make use of truth. We must develop a comprehensive, abiding, and systematic understanding of the failure of information assimilation.

Ramachandran observes this failure of information integration and asks how the mind can be so insistent in its denial of information that is plainly visible? Clearly not all information in memory is available for thought at all times. What makes information assimilation possible at times and impossible at other times? Researchers in many fields have begun to address this problem. Keith Stenning has worked in the field of cognitive science to understand the emotional processes of thought. He argues that "information consumption" is not a straightforward procedure. Not all information can be taken in. "The process of internalization has to connect with what is already there," he says (Stenning 2002, 5). Ramachandran and Stenning demonstrate a general principle. It is foolish to assume that people can easily take in information—even when it is crucial to their well-being. The mind is not a computer that instantly makes use of information. The mind is often more like a thirsty mule, unwilling to drink even when it has been brought to the water. It would be in the "best interest" of anosognosia patients to understand their bodily limits. But this need for knowledge is defeated by what seems to be an attachment to established beliefs.

It is crucial for educators to understand the various patterns and styles of denial. But we will learn more from Ramachandran than from Fish. Fish is memorable for his alarming generalizations: Minds are not responsive to evidence. Ramachandran is most compelling in terms of the irrefutable evidence of his findings. He demonstrates, on the one hand, a degree of denial that most of us would not have thought possible, the hallucination of evidence. And, on the other hand, he gives examples of people overcoming their denial and accepting evidence through a process no one would have dreamed effective, the overcoming of denial through rapid eye movement (REM), the kind of brain activity we typically see in dreaming. It is as if we dream our way into responsible thinking.

Unconscious Integrated and Unintegrated Knowledge

Ramachandran's anosognosia patients demonstrate a crucial feature of the resistance to "irrefutable facts" not recognized by Fish. Some of the information refuted by resistant thinkers is in fact in their minds. It is just that it is not yet integrated with their reason. It is present unconsciously, but it has not been "assimilated" by processes that allow a conscious mind to make use of information present in short term memory.

Ramachandran found his patients would recognize their paralysis if he triggered REM by injecting cold water into their ear canal. After he has administered the water, he asks one patient if she can use both arms. At this moment she changes her response and replies, "No my left arm is paralyzed." Ramachandran observes:

> This is an extraordinary remark, for it implies that even though she had been denying her paralysis each time I had seen her over these last few weeks, the memories of her failed attempts had been registering somewhere in her brain, yet access to them had been blocked. (1999, 146)

After the eye movement has had an effect on brain function, the woman does not even need to see the inability of her arm to act. She remembers it; she had in reality "seen" it all along. This information is stored in the woman's mind, in her "memory," but her conscious thinking mind cannot make use of the memory until the cold water triggers REM, integrates memory, and changes how her mind functions.

Ramachadran speculates that the waking REM, similar to the REM of dreams, "internalizes" information stored in memory but not used by memory. These minds already "know" this information, but these same minds, while they "have information," are unable to consciously and verbally testify to it.

This book will be about a subjective state I have decided to describe as "the desire not to know." I am borrowing this phrase from the work of British psychiatrist Wilfred Bion who theorized that some responses of the mind to information involve an act of avoidance. He represented this movement of mind in shorthand as "–K" (Bion 1959). I am uncomfortable with Ramachandran's term "denial." Though Freud coined the term to mean an unconscious act, it generally implies in everyday usage a willful, conscious act. People "in denial" often seem to express a stubborn willfulness. Rather than use the term "denial," I will cautiously employ a more awkward term, "the desire not to know." This is not a perfect phrase as it may imply a conscious experience of desire. In most cases I do not think there is conscious awareness of a desire to "not know." Nonetheless the term does imply an emotional motive for denial rather than a response guided by will or reason. If we can recognize the desire not to know as emotional, we may be more inclined to respond according to an emotional rather than a cognitive logic.

The examples of the desire not to know that I am taking from the work of V. S. Ramachandran illustrate both the unimaginable reach of this principle and the possible solution to the problem. The cold water experiment proves that information can be unconsciously "taken in" by a mind but not fully assimilated into conscious thinking. Concerted attempts to "point" to the evidence of immediate perception seem to have no effect in integrating evidence with reason. But other practices that address not the evidence but the workings of memory and emotion in the mind, do integrate the evidence.

Western universities are very adept at the production of information. We seem to have almost no understanding of the "consumption" or "assimilation of information." We often assume, as Ken Bain points out, that if we teach information, we will produce students who can use information. We find countless examples that contradict this assumption. But by and large we continue to test for skills and neglect the crucial issues of the mind's development and assimilation of information as a problem-solving process.

Universities devote enormous resources to the production of information but almost no resources to the assimilation of information. We know that such disregard is enormously costly. But faced with the evidence of the desire not to know, we act as if humans are rational. When we observe evidence to the contrary we are, like Ramachandran and the education researchers, "astonished." We are astonished over and over again without apparently learning anything. Our astonishment testifies to our desire not to know how minds characteristically fail to incorporate uncomfortable information.

Our astonishment shuts down our own thinking about minds. We see evidence of what we do not want to believe, but our disbelief undoes our thinking at exactly the point where we need to be more thoughtful and active.

The rejection of evidence is perhaps the most costly cause of human folly. We must, first, understand the enormity of the problem, and, second, understand that we can remedy the problem. Peter Kline and Bernard Saunders point out that "training and education can be so conducted that no learning takes place" (2010, 63). Schools usually "test" students' learning by asking them to pass tests demonstrating what they have learned. The work of Halloun and Hestenes shows that students can pass tests that "prove" that they have been trained even though they have not learned anything. American education, I would argue, seldom grasps the difference between training and learning. And as long as educational systems test for training as opposed to learning, we spend vast sums of money to justify our own "everyday unimaginable stupidity."

Information, Memory, and the Neuroscience of the Unconscious

To understand how information is used by brains, we must understand how information is stored in memory. We must understand, in addition, how memory is used (and not used) by brains to solve problems.

Training gets information into a mind. Simple tests can determine if minds "contain" or remember information. But if education only puts information into minds, it does noting to insure that people can develop the emotional flexibility to solve problems with information. Ramachandran, along with neurobiologists Joseph LeDoux, and

Antonio Damasio inform us of complex relations among information, emotion, memory, and problem solving (Damasio 1995, 1999, 2003, 2012; LeDoux 1998; Ramachandran 1999, 2012). People can have conscious awareness of information that they make no use of and people can, in an inverse manner, make use of information that they have no conscious awareness of.

Educators must do more to develop, not the verbal logical mind, but the nonverbal, emotional, and unconscious mind. The production of information without the assimilation of information is a foolish and fruitless endeavor. Universities must take responsibility for understanding the processes of assimilation of information. We must explore teaching practices, similar to the REMs that can contribute to better information assimilation.

We must promote an educational experiential equivalent of dreaming—educational practices that facilitate emotional and memorial reorganization. When Ramachandran uses REMs to integrate information within the brain of his patient, he is contributing to something I am calling the "emotional assimilation of thought." I will use this term in each chapter and I will describe the social, psychological, and emotional activities that contribute to and impede these processes. I will use research in the sciences to support my more controversial claims. I will use examples from the classroom and from scholarly interaction to illustrate my ideas.[2]

The unconscious has recently become an important concept in the neurosciences. Antonio Damasio explains, "The unconscious, in the narrow meaning in which the word has been etched in our culture, is only part of the vast amount of processes and contents that remain nonconscious" (Damasio 1999, 228). I would advise any reader not comfortable with the term (belief can always be an obstacle to understanding) to examine the considerable research that now greatly clarifies the workings of the unconscious and the nonconscious.

Ramachandran's account of various forms of biological blindness is particularly impressive. One patient, Diane, wakes up from a coma completely blind. She was, we are told, "blind in every traditional sense of the word" (Ramachandran 1999, 64). In working with Dr. David Milner, a neuropsychologist at the University of St. Andrews, however, Diane shows an "astonishing" ability to orient her hands and body perfectly in relation to objects that she cannot see. She is able to "deftly" take a pencil from Dr. Milner's hand, and she is able to adroitly rotate a letter with perfect precision in relation to a mail slot that she cannot see it. There is a brain inside Diane working with information from her visual field, Ramachandran tell us. It is simply that Diane has no conscious awareness of how her unconscious brain is working. She acts, the information is "processed," but it is never consciously recognized. Diane, like most people, but much more dramatically than most people, makes use of unconscious knowledge to act in the world.

Antonio Damasio lists five kinds of information that are fully operative but not consciously perceived. This information can be internal images or sensations that are present in the brain but not present to consciousness. It can be remembered emotional states that are present but not active in consciousness. I will give emphasis to four of these information types:

> 1. all the fully formed images to which we do not attend; 2. all the neural patterns that never become images; 3. all the dispositions which were acquired through experience, lie dormant, and may never become a neural pattern; 4. all the quiet remodeling of such dispositions and their quiet networking—that never may become explicitly known. (Damasio 1999, 228)

We might posit that the anosognosia patient who fails to see the paralysis in her arm owns an unconscious containing "neural patterns that never become images" and "fully formed images to which" she does not attend. To know the information about her paralysis, her brain has to do "work" on her unconscious. This work would require what Damasio terms "the quiet remodeling of such dispositions" that impede awareness of uncomfortable information.

Political commentator David Brooks sums up a vast amount of current research that testifies to the importance of the unconscious in human thought:

> We are living in the middle of a revolution in consciousness. Over the past few years, geneticists, neuroscientists, psychologists, sociologists, economists, anthropologists, and others have made great strides in understanding the building blocks of human flourishing. And a core finding of their work is that we are not primarily the products of our conscious thinking. We are primarily the products

of thinking that happens below the level of awareness. (Brooks, 2012, viii)

A key principle for educators is the fact that minds are not machines that effortlessly run the logic of verbal consciousness. Damasio offers a careful observation of the difference between linguistic consciousness and mind:

> On several occasions when I was in medical school and in neurology training, I remember asking some of the wisest people around me how we produced the conscious mind. Curiously, I always got the same answer: language did it. I was told that creatures without language were limited to their uncognizant existence but not we fortunate humans because language made us know. Consciousness was a verbal interpretation of ongoing mental processes. (Damasio 1999, 107)

This last claim is important in relation to Ramachandran's patient who denies that the arm attached to her body is her own arm. We imagine the mind to be a "verbal interpretation of ongoing mental processes"; we expect this woman to be "centered" in a mind that is itself "centered" in the secure ground of responsible verbal reasoning and awareness of a shared visible world. The doctor points to a shared world, "this arm is attached to your body," and he invites a logical verbal response linked to his own reasoning and observation. The patient's response to the doctor should be, "Of course this is my arm." But although the doctor can situate the reference "this arm" in a variety of verbal contexts that would seem to "lead" inevitably to a recognition of "this arm" as a meaning made real by "ongoing mental processes," the linguistic sentence "this is my arm" and its accompanying thought is never formulated. The woman insists that the arm attached to her body is not her arm.

Her mind, clearly, is doing something else. Her mind does not reflect the relationship to visual perception, language, and intersubjective interaction we expect. Her mind is not a "verbal interpretation of ongoing mental process" as we normally understand those processes. Her mind is a reflection of unconscious processes comfortably in denial of perception, logic, and their impact of truth claims.

We respond to a person's mind as "present" because of how it responds to language. This patient is talking to the doctor. She shows she understands the meaning of words. She seems sane in every respect but one. Her use of language in relation to the doctor demonstrates the presence of a "sound" mind. But at a particular point in her use of language, her mind apparently "fails" to operate.

Most of us, when we encounter someone who denies what seems obvious, attempt to reason the person to the conclusions we find obvious. Equally often, though, we continue to reason with this person past a point where we feel utility in our reasoning. Our reasonableness then turns to irritation. We seem to experience a moral shortcoming in this person, a "bullheadedness" that seems determined to do something wrong or harmful. Some people, perhaps, feel that anger can be a cause for increasing the capacities for rationality in another. To be angry with such a mind is like kicking a car for not starting. You may experience satisfaction by releasing your frustration, but you do nothing to improve the mechanical condition of the car.

We may think of reason as an essential power of the mind expressed in language. The clarity of language gives us access to an apparent "force" of reason. But minds are not machines run on reason. Minds are housed in brains that operate according to altogether different principles. Damasio's work with brain damaged patients demonstrates that people who lose the capacity for language do not lose a highly precise ability to think. There is a "mental relation" to the world in these brain damaged patients, but this relation is not grounded in the system and logic of language. Damasio explains,

> As I studied case after case of patients with severe language disorders caused by neurological diseases, I realized that no matter how much impairment of language there was, the patient's thought processes remained intact in their essentials. (1999, 108)

Processes of human thought can work independent of language. People who lose the ability to use language still have the ability to reason. Damasio points out: "In every instance I know...People function with full 'presence of mind' and understanding of the world. So what is going on if not the use of language?" (1999, 109). If people are not grounded in the world through language, we should not expect an insistence on language to sharpen their understanding of the world. Repeating the logic of a certain verbal understanding of the world does not deliver that understanding to the inner world of the person addressed.

Feelings as Organizers and Predispositions for Knowledge

The core of mind, Damasio proposes, operates as feeling. Feelings can be made present to consciousness in terms of what he terms "images." The brain is run by emotion, not by consciousness. This means that even when we believe that we determine our lives consciously, we are unconscious of emotional experiences that orchestrate what becomes conscious. He observes:

> The fabric of our minds and of our behavior is woven around continuous cycles of emotions followed by feelings that become known and beget new emotions, a running polyphony that underscores and punctuates specific thoughts in our minds and actions in our behavior. (Damasio 1999, 43)

Minds are, at the core, "continuous cycles of emotions followed by feelings that become known." We inevitably see our minds from the outside, in terms of the feelings that become known. What we do not see is the "running polyphony" that bring inner feelings into verbal testimony and recognition.

Damasio proposes that the complex "extended consciousness" we see as mind reflects a deeper emotionally organized experience of self he terms "core consciousness":

> Core consciousness includes an inner sense based on images... The particular images are those of a feeling. That inner sense conveys a powerful nonverbal message regarding the relationship between the organism and the object. (1999, 125)

Relationships between "the organism" and "the object" are subject to filters determined by networks of feeling. New information can be made available to consciousness, but not all new information is integrated within the biology of the brain so that conscious thought has free use of pertinent information. In the case of Ramachandran's anosognosia patients, the mind maintains the self as consistent and unchanged—even when the body has been changed.

Ramachandran proposes that the two halves of the brain play different roles in responding to new information. The left brain remembers and maintains a stable sense of self and body. The right brain makes changes to this schema of self and body when such changes are necessary. This ongoing process of mind is biologically complex: "At any given moment in our waking lives, our brains are flooded with a bewildering array of sensory inputs, all of which must be incorporated into a coherent perspective that's based on what our stored memories already tell us is true about ourselves and the world" (Ramachandran 1999, 134). As the basic principle of mind requires the reproduction of the sense of self and new adjustments to the sense of self, there are occasions of conflict between the past self, seeking to continue as it is, and present information that would alter established assumptions.

Ramachandran suggests that

> the coping strategies of the two hemispheres are fundamentally different. The left hemisphere's job is to create a belief system or model and to fold new experiences into that belief system. If confronted with some new information that doesn't fit the model, it relies on Freudian defense mechanisms to deny, repress or confabulate—anything to preserve the status quo. (1999, 136)

This adjusting of self to world takes place, first of all, "unconsciously," that is to say outside our conscious awareness, and second, on the basis of "feeling." Information from the outer world need not be compelling. For most of us, the mind works on the principle of "autopilot" and unconsciously filters out much new information. Timothy Wilson explains:

> The mind operates most efficiently by relegating a good deal of high-level, sophisticated thinking to the unconscious, just as a modern jumbo jetliner is able to fly on automatic pilot with little or no input from the human, "conscious" pilot. The adaptive unconscious does an excellent job of sizing up the world, warning people of danger, setting goals, and initiating action in a sophisticated and efficient manner. (2002, 97–99)

All this research suggests that much of the content of our life is organized unconsciously along emotional principles. New information that introduces significant conflict within an existing emotional/feeling system is not integrated with the reasoning resources of the brain.

Current research in neurobiology suggests that the assimilation of new information requires emotional integration and readjustment. We can promote reason only when we understand how to "dream" our way into emotional integration. In making this very paradoxical argument I will be synthesizing the implications of Ramachandran's experiments with much scientific research on minds, brains, and consciousness. Before I discuss the "emotional assimilation of knowledge," though, I want to address a persistent problem researchers encounter in talking about this problem of denial.

The Disbelief of Denial: How We Continue to Believe in Reason

My argument about the human failure to take in information has two parts. The first part of the argument calls attention to the many kinds of evidence that come from medicine, politics, education, clinical practice, and everyday life. We have many examples of people failing to take in information. The second part of my argument, however, is concerned with our own inability to take in information *about* our inability to take in information. We see the event, we are momentarily stunned, but we then continue to think very much as we had before. We see unreason and then insist that people can and should be reasonable.

Ramachandran says, "Talking to denial patients can be an uncanny experience. They bring us face to face with some of the most fundamental questions one can ask as a conscious human being." If we think of consciousness as inherently an awareness of the world and other people, Ramachandran's patients force us to revise our understanding of consciousness. When he describes his encounter with denial as an experience of the "uncanny," he expresses very precisely a common response that both recognizes and dismisses the problem at the same time.

The uncanny is an experience that shakes us to the core. Japanese engineers working with life like robots have developed the concept of an "uncanny valley" to describe gradations in the characteristic human response to lifelike figures (Saygin 2011). Freud used the

German word "uncanny" (roughly translated as "unhomelike") to describe an experience revealing something threatening in the visage of something familiar (homelike). Ramachandran sees a mind. Our minds are our homes. To see an uncanny mind, then, is to see a "homelike" mind as very disturbing.

In reporting his "disbelief," Ramachandran points out that even though he directly sees what is happening, he cannot believe it. But at precisely this point Ramachandran's own mind operates like his patient's mind. Just as the denial patient cannot believe that her arm is paralyzed, so also Ramachandran cannot believe that a mind can be so paralyzed. Just as the patient is "in denial" about the powers of her arm, Ramachandran is "in denial" about the power of the human mind. Ramachandran's "disbelief" reenacts, within his own mind, the inability to take in the objective truth that he observes in the other mind.

I will be referring repeatedly to this subjective experience of the recognition of the mind's refutation of "irrefutable evidence" in the present book. People see an example of a mind in an action of "denial"—and they are "astonished." They are just not prepared to assimilate what they see. It is as if we hold an assumption about the mind's rationality, we then see an example of thinking that contradicts out assumption, and yet we maintain our disproved assumption. We see evidence of the mind's ability to refute "irrefutable evidence," but then, rather than change our assumptions about rationality, we continue to believe in the force of reason. We continue to be "astonished" over and over again as we repeatedly see instances of denial. We are like Fish's "true believers" in our attachment to a false understanding of the mind. We can't take in the evidence of our senses.

Ramachandran, unlike many researchers, took his disbelief seriously. He decided to explore what this event might mean. He attempted a few tests to see how denial worked. Initially he decided to test his own disbelief. Perhaps what he saw was not a failure of mind, but a shrewd cunning. Perhaps these patients really could see their arms' paralysis, but for various reasons pretended not to. He tested this possibility with an ingenious experiment. He placed a glass of water on a tray directly opposite the paralyzed arm. He reasoned that if the patient really knew that his arm was paralyzed he would do one of two things on being presented with the tray. Either he would hold the tray in the middle with his one good hand in order to avoid spilling the water, or he would make an excuse for why he could not take the tray. Instead of these responses, Ramachandran found that these patients held out their (one) good arm, and then, because only one arm was holding the tray, the tray tilted and the water spilled on the floor. Confronted with the spilled water, they continue to deny their paralysis. They always fabricated an explanation, "My hand slipped." They did not recognize their paralyzed arm. Ramachandran was astonished.

When I teach Ramachandran to my graduate students, they too are astonished. Astonishment is an interesting emotional response to this simple factual event. Why do we experience a profound emotional disturbance in this event? We are presented with a simple observation. People exhibit behavior that purports to be "thought" but is obviously not thought. "Thought" in this case represents precisely an inability to think. We have an apparently sane woman claim her arms works, or point to her own arm and claim that it is her brother's arm. And yet this fact, this act of witnessing that we are presented with, is something we ourselves cannot take in as information. Our emotional response betrays our inability to fully pursue the implications.

Just as the woman cannot acknowledge the loss of her arm, we cannot acknowledge the woman's loss of reason. Our response is similar to Ramachandran's first response. When Ramachandran first witnesses the event, he feels disbelief. Just as the woman denies the disability of her arm, Ramachandran denies (in that moment of face-to-face talk) the disability of the human mind. He says he "cannot believe" what she is saying. The mind's essential disability, though factually visible, cannot be assimilated as thought.

You too are implicated in this story. What Ramachandran demonstrates is an insult to cherished ideas we have about the mind's powers. All of us, like Ramachandran, want to refuse to deny, dismiss, or forget the story this knowledge tells us about our minds. We insist upon seeing our minds as heroic witnesses to truth, when in fact they are characteristically paralyzed and disabled by ideals and beliefs that are emotionally uncomfortable.

In recent years research in political science reflects a similar astonishment regarding the minds of American voters. Joe Keohane represents these finding in an aptly titled article, "How Facts Backfire, Researchers Discover a Surprising Threat to Democracy: Our Brains." Writing for the *Boston Globe*, on July 11, 2010, Keohane summarizes a number of research findings that indicate that not only are American voters surprisingly ignorant of key facts in world and national affairs, but attempts to correct them frequently lead to a "backfire affect." Instead of taking in the facts and changing their beliefs, they insist all the more strongly on what they believe to be true. The "force" placed on their minds by reasonable evidence is denied by a resistant force from within them. When given creditable evidence about the world, they desire not to know it. They continue to believe what they want more vigorously when the preponderance of the evidence suggests that such information is false.

The desire to support a belief contrary to evidence and reason has not been ignored by historians, philosophers, and rhetoricians. Political scientist Drew Westen argues in *The Political Brain*:

> The notion that people can unconsciously protect themselves against threatening information has a venerable history... philosophers (not to mention playwrights and poets) have known about this quality of the human mind for centuries. It was central to Freud's thinking over a century ago. In more recent years, researchers have documented self-serving "reasoning" in a range of domains, including politics. (2007, 100)

Barbara Herrnstein Smith, in *Belief and Resistance*, points out that even strong material disincentives to belief do not release individuals from tenacious commitments to established belief:

> Human history indicates that people will maintain their beliefs not only in the face of apparently contrary evidence but even when those beliefs have severely disagreeable and disadvantageous consequences for them—not to mention for many other people. (1997, 51)

We have known about this quality of human denial for a long time, but most of us act just like people informed of their mistakes. We notice peoples' inability to take information, and but we keep faith in the transformative value of information itself.

In response to encounters with the denial of facts, people do not come to understand that human do not take in facts. Instead they seek to more urgently produce and publish facts. We see people not taking in facts, and our response is simply to insist more emphatically upon the facts. The Annenberg Public Policy Center maintains

FactCheck.org. *The Washington Post* runs a Fact Checker column. George Washington University has sponsored a project "Face the Facts" with the purpose "to help American's debunk myths, hold better conversations, get involved, and make choices as smarter citizens" (http://www.facethefactsusa.org). We seem unable to face the facts about our inability to take in facts.

Part of the problem of thinking about the problem is an inability to imagine a solution. Possible solutions to the problem seem absurd or outlandish. Ramachandran's experiments suggest that REM activity integrates memory and overcomes emotional resistance to thought. How can we think about this? How can this "work" be imagined as an educational process?

On the Emotional Assimilation of Knowledge

New and uncomfortable information cannot be integrated without what I term the "emotional assimilation" of such information. Uncomfortable information cannot be taken in easily because it requires changes in the organization of the emotional body of the self. Existing feeling states and memories create conditions such that uncomfortable information cannot be stored in memory effectively. New but unpleasant information is doomed to remain stranded in unavailable memory unless work is done on what LeDoux calls the "emotional implications" of memory.

Research in many disciplines now emphasizes a necessary interrelationship between reason and emotion. Reason can incorporate uncomfortable information. But this process does not take place in an instant of rational thought and it does not take place by a process of rational thought. Integration is accomplished through the processing of emotional experience. Cognitive scientist Kenneth Stenning argues:

> Affective structure is instrumental in determining what we learn, and how we subsequently deploy it... It is instrumental in determining what we learn both as a precondition for learning and because it is what comes to implement the new capacities which constitute our learning. (2002, 258)

Emotion gives meaning to meaning. Ideas have value in relation to affective consequences. Thoughts "strike us" with affective resonance.

We anticipate a world informed by feeling states organized by past memories. New information cannot shape habits of mind until it is integrated within a preexisting affective network. Meanings not yet affectively integrated have no real purchase on thought.

Damasio explains how his understanding of reason changed through his study of the brain damaged, nineteenth-century railroad worker Phineas Gage. An accident transformed Gage from a man fully responsible and reasonable, before his accident, to a man unable to manage life tasks afterward. Damasio reasoned that the accident damaged brain centers that allowed emotion to be processed. He came to revise his fundamental understanding about reason. He states, "I had been advised early in life that sound decisions came from a cool head, that reason and emotion did not mix any more than oil and water" (Damasio 1995 xii). He learned from Gage that thought without emotion cannot be rational in any practical sense. Gage could calculate the sum of numbers very effectively, but he could not make rational life decisions.

Stenning summarizes Damasio with the observation: "Real-world reasoning, as distinct from the solution of laboratory puzzles, needs affect for effective control" (2002, 261). Damasio (1995, 1999) argues that thought affecting human action is always grounded in networks of emotion—hope, fear, suspicion, pride, shame, enthusiasm. John Cacioppo, in *Foundations in Social Neuroscience*, sums up much research in neuroscience when he points out that "affect directs attention, guides decision making, stimulates learning and triggers behavior" (Cacioppo et al. 2002, 494). Emotional bias may be bad for rationality. But bias is bad not because of emotion; it is bad because it misrepresents necessary relations between emotion and thought. Bias reflects limited emotional contexts that are too quickly brought to bear on the implication of thought. Reason reflects thought that has explored meaning in relation to multiple but real emotional contexts.

In the case of Ramachandran's patients with anosognosia, the missing information about injury can be recognized by the mind under three conditions that change its emotional context but do not change its biological condition.

One condition for taking in the information was very simple. Ramachandran found he could "gently prod" some patients into "eventually admitting" that an arm was "weak" or "not working" or, in the best of cases, "paralyzed." He points out that doctors normally do not want to do this because patients become very upset. He risks this response, however, and talks to a particular woman over a long period of time, insisting that what she believes is in fact not true. In the case reported, the woman admits to the recognition and then has what medical doctors call a "catastrophic" response: She cries for ten minutes. She then admits that she knows her arm is paralyzed. We might imagine, in this context, that what is at stake for this woman is not knowledge, but pain and loss. We can well imagine that pain and loss make some thoughts unthinkable.

We would hope the gentle prodding achieves results. But Ramachandran reports that this recognition is temporary. When he leaves the room and returns ten minutes later, this woman has no memory of her recognition of paralysis. Under pressure, she was pushed to bring the recognition to consciousness. But she very soon forgets any such event. I am writing this book because a very similar event happened to me in the classroom. My class, through my gentle and clever prodding, accepted a general claim one day and then had no memory of their own thinking in the subsequent class meeting. This story is chapter two of the present book. I was so astonished by the event that I have spent ten years trying to make sense of it.

Ramachandran considered denial as having a psychological motivation. It may be a response to threat. He formulated a strategy to test psychological conditions under which the right brain can take in information about the paralysis of the body. He reasons: "What if we could somehow make this 'unpleasant' fact more acceptable— more nonthreatening to a patient's belief system? Would he then be willing to accept that his left arm is paralyzed? In other words, can you 'cure' his denial by simply tampering with the structure of his beliefs?" (Ramachandran 1999, 151). In order to test this "what if" hypothesis, Ramachandran selects patients in denial and tells them that he will inject an anesthetic in their left arm. Under these temporary conditions, their arm will not be able to function. In reality, he injects, not an anesthetic, but a harmless saline solution. The patient now "believes" that their left arm is "temporarily" paralyzed. He then asks them if they can move their arm. They attempt to move their arm and perceive that it will not move. They then report that indeed their left arm is paralyzed. Information denial caused purportedly by tissue damage is now accepted without healing or repair.

In a case such as this, it would seem that what is at stake for the mind is not the paralysis of the arm, but what it means emotionally for the arm to be paralyzed. The individual "cannot accept" a permanent condition of paralysis. Thus whatever it is they have to believe for the purposes of denial, they confirm by acts of "seeing," even if evidence in the real world contradicts what they want to see. They will argue vehemently with people who see the world "objectively."

Ramachandran decides to test for a possible "hypnotic" effect of his presence. He tries the same test on the patient's right arm, which in fact operates effectively. In this case the patient is told their right arm will be left temporarily paralyzed by the experiment. After the injection the patient is asked if they can move their right arm. They discover that, although they expected their right arm to be paralyzed, it is not. They are not moved by suggestions to confirm whatever their doctor tells them. Ramachandran rules out the "hypnotic suggestion" explanation of the cure. By providing a change in the emotional implications of a fact, Ramachandran shows how a previously unassimilated fact can become assimilated. This example supports Damasio's claim that reason relies upon emotion to determine what kinds of "representations" can be entertained and worked with.

Ramachandran's most interesting remedy for the denial of paralysis remains the work done by REM. This was a remedy that survived subsequent re-denials and did not require lying. It is both the most interesting remedy and the most difficult to understand. Ramachandran notes that his use of cold water to recover knowledge of disability was something long known to medical doctors, but largely neglected. The results of the experiment had extraordinary implications, but no one seemed to grasp the implications. He says:

> Here was a neurological syndrome produced by a right parietal lesion that had been reversed by the simple act of squirting water into the ear. Why hadn't this amazing experiment made headlines in the *New York Times*? Indeed I discovered that most of my professional colleagues had not even heard of the experiment. (Ramachandran 1999, 144)

Why weren't people more interesting in "thinking" about this discovery? Thinking about this would seem to be important, and yet people seem unable to imagine what is at stake in understanding. Perhaps once again, we see a human tendency to not want to know how the mind works.

Ramachandran's cold water experiment repeated work done in 1987 by Italian neurologist Edoardo Bisiach. Bisiach discovered that if he irrigated (squirted water from a syringe) a denial person's ear canal with cold water, the denial symptoms would disappear. The cold water affects the ear canal and prompts the brain to experience movement in the head. This imagined perception of movement in the head generates REMs. Under this condition the patient can perceive what they had earlier denied.

Ramachandran offers a speculative explanation of this remedy: "I suggest that the vestibular stimulation caused by the cold water partially activates the same circuitry that generates REM sleep. This allows the patient to uncover unpleasant, disturbing facts about herself—including her paralysis—that are usually repressed when she is awake" (1999, 147). Ramachandran links REM activity to memory consolidation in dreams. It is now possible to compare his results with the results obtained currently by the use of EMDR (eye movement desensitization and reprocessing) trauma therapy. EMDR began as an accidental discovery that eye movement could be stimulated and used effectively in trauma therapy for the synthesis of dissociated memory. Although the procedure sounds implausible, the results have proven highly beneficial (Seidler and Wagner 2006). In both EMDR therapy and Ramachandran's water irrigation technique, left and right eye movement seems to integrate memory.

Research suggests REM sleep is responsible for the consolidation of new learning into long-term memory (Cartwright 2004). Daniel Siegel describes REM activity in sleep as significantly altering relations existing among memory and emotion. REM sleep rearranges or "consolidates" relations among various elements' stored memory: "Consolidation appears to involve the reorganization of existing memory traces" (Siegel 1999, 37). Reorganization changes both the content and internal relations of memory. There are new links between elements already in memory but not linked, and there is modification of existing memory content as the result of new links. Siegel explains that "consolidation may make new associational linkages, condense elements of memory into new clusters of representation, and incorporate previously unintegrated elements into a functional whole" (1999, 37).

Dreams are often experienced as bizarrely associated images and feelings. Neurological research describes dreaming as a brain activity that integrates new psychic material within established and also newly evolving pathways of neural links and relations (Cartwright 2004; Payne and Nadel 2004; Revonsuo 2000; Foulkes 1999; Solms 1995, 1997). Dreams help us make sense of a new experience by reviving an old experience, but they also do the reverse—they make sense of an old experience by connecting it to a new experience. The meaning of the past changes so that this remembered past, which is the condition of our emotional anticipation or interpretive "bias" toward the future, becomes modified. Changes in the meanings of our past change our ability to imagine a future.

Dreams integrate a new experience to established memories and facilitate experimental associative patterns. Often dream content suggests meanings just outside of currently coherent verbal summary. Siegel proposes that we can think of these experiences as the "work" of the "dream" to "make sense of recent experience" (1999, 37). Ramachandran's patient makes sense of her own recent experience of body loss through REM activity. Her REM has allowed her, as Siegel says to "incorporate previously unintegrated elements into a functional whole." She can, in effect, reason with her whole mind, making use of the "irrefutable information" she had earlier refuted.

Observing Minds That Desire Not to Know

Minds may take in information, only to store it in memory locations where it is not utilized. Understanding the brain's biology allows us more insight into the mind's behavior. If we turn our gaze from the biology of the brain to the narrative of the mind, Wilfred Bion offers helpful observations and concepts for understanding these events. Bion describes the desire not to know from the perspective of a therapist who observes the step-by-step process of thought and denial in a therapy patient. Bion noted how a certain developing process of logical thought would veer away from an effective problem-solving logic because of a variety of disabling emotions such as anxiety, fear, anger, or shame. If a mind thinks of new information, and in that moment experiences anxiety, fear, anger, or shame, that new information may not be effectively integrated.

Established networks of feeling impede the assimilation of information. New information that would cause severe emotional pain or would drastically reorganize an established system of thought is turned from integration.

Bion's empirical observations of a mind involved in a series of linking events we describe as "thought" helps us to understand from the inside what Ramachandran sees in his anosognosia patients on the outside. If we look at this like Bion, we are not scientists considering how the biological brain impedes information assimilation. We are trained observers looking at the sequential steps of a thought process in a particular mind. Both perspectives are objective observations of empirical behavior. Both perspectives can help teachers understand how students deny information.

Part of Bion's argument about the work of the mind is that "links" in thought are determined by emotion. People who feel a great deal of hate about a subject are not easily able to make a "thoughtful" link to information that requires an opposite emotional feeling about that same subject. Emotion, not logic, drives patterns of linked thoughts. In chapter two I will discuss in more detail Bion's account of minds functioning in terms of "logics" of hate or love, the primary emotions that restrict what is attended to, organize what is perceived, and interpret what is thought. If Bion had been a rhetorician he might have phrased the problem much like Fish: "True belief does not emerge from reason's chain; rather true belief—and false belief too—configure reason's chain" (Fish 2001, 501). Instead of talking about chains of reason and discourse communities, Bion focused sharply on the emotional ground and motive for "reason's chains." Links in thought are formed into "chains" driven by our loves and our hates.

My own primary training in psychology, literature, philosophy, and psychoanalysis has been focused on the processes of mind, not on the biological processes of the brain. I find Bion's vocabulary and style of observation compatible with my own. I have come to believe, however, that it is important to have an understanding of the biology of the brain. If we better understand the biology of thought, we can better understand why the mind behaves as it does. The mind is limited in its a functioning by the brain's biology. Integrated thought requires integration of many aspects of memory, emotion, and problem solving. Emotional states powerfully influence memory retrieval (Damasio 1999). Prefrontal lobe thought is not possible under conditions of acute fear. Anxiety can generate "defensive responses" that preclude access to particular memories. Associations that trigger the primitive neural structures of the brain, such as the amygdala, cannot be contained by processes we call "reason." Information with varying degrees of emotional intensity and context is stored in different brain areas and it can be "retrieved" only under particular conditions. Computers may instantly compute information. Brains and minds do not.

Information that makes us emotionally uncomfortable is never taken in easily. Uncomfortable information is experienced first not as information, but as a desire not to know. The desire not to know ranges from very dramatic cases, as in the situation of patients with anosognosia, to everyday unrealistic idealizations as described by Katherine Anne Porter's narrator in "Old Morality." A father in the story tells his daughters, "There were never any fat women in the family, thank God." Porter's narrator reports the daughters' thought: "Well, Great-Aunt Keziah was famous for her heft, and wasn't she in the family? But something seemed to happen to their father's memory when he thought of the girls he had known in the family of his youth, and he declared steadfastly they had all been without exception as slim as reeds and as graceful as sylphs" (Porter [1936] 1962, 11). The refutation of evidence here seems very slight, perhaps even admirable. But one can imagine that if this tendency to idealization shifts from the family to one's political party, then the implications become more serious.

One particular feature in this fictional account of the desire not to know has useful implications. Why does the father "think" that all the women in the family had been "without exception" slim? Why isn't it enough to simply say, "They had all been slim." This need to give emphasis precisely to the point where the denial is a lie represents an important marker of the desire not to know. One of Ramachandran's patients with anosognosia insists that he enjoys "two-fisted" drinking. Ramachandran wonders why he wants to talk about drinking as involving "two fists." Why is there this insistence on a level of detail, "without exception" and "two-fisted," that adds no information to a communication except to emphasize a denial? In one case a patient says, "I tied my shoelaces with both my hands" (Ramachandran 1999, 143). We don't normally say this. Usually a person would say, "I tied my shoelaces." It is only in a condition of denial that a person adds detail to emphasize the insistence on the lie—"I tied my shoelaces with both my hands." Situations of denial are often marked by expressions of oddly emphatic insistence. Here, as elsewhere, gaps in thought that might be determined by logic are replaced by links in thought determined by emotion.

Novelist J. G. Farrell observes a mind that recognizes its own fear of information as having the potential to disrupt an internal emotional organization. He describes the thinking of a Japanese soldier during the World War II invasion of Singapore thus.

> Kikuchi was astonished and awed by Lieutenant Matsusita. Every time he met those burning eyes it was as if he received an electric shock. The intensity of feeling in Matsusita, his utter devotion to the emperor and to his country... Yet there was something that Kikuchi found rather frightening about him at the same time... Sometimes it almost seemed as if he wanted to get not only himself but everyone else killed too.
>
> The thought had crossed Kikuchi's mind—indeed it had to be frogmarched across his mind under heavy guard and swiftly, like a deserter who must not be allowed to contaminate his fellows—that all things in human affairs, even battlefield glory, can be taken a bit too far. (Farrell 1973, 371)

Farrell reveals an emerging thought that violates an existing network of strong emotional attachments. This soldier finds himself in a new but highly emotional context. He is in danger of being killed. This powerful new emotional context—the immediate threat of death—demands revisionary thought. Why is he in this condition? What might he do to solve his problem? He has a thought that might save his life. But this thought would have logical implications. It would modify the enthusiasm of his loyalty to his leader.

Thoughts such as this can emerge in consciousness. But they are not "easy" thoughts to think. They are thoughts that disturb other thoughts. Such thought must be carefully controlled. Farrell's soldier fears that this emergent thought may "contaminate" other thoughts—that is, organize them into a logical network of thought that threatens established patterns of feeling and behavior. In this example, the thought might lead the soldier to distrust Matsusita, his commanding officer. If this thought were to emerge fully acknowledged, it might lead logically to another thought—that it is in fact foolish to follow Matsusita unquestioningly. But this next step in logic is carefully forestalled.

We would want Kikuchi to follow up on his thinking, to actively question his blind obedience. But if Kikuchi is to think further, he must take up a complex and painful emotional task. He must experience a network of emotions and particular sites of memory that give meaning to his understanding of loyalty, honor, and self-identity. He must reflect on the conflict between his fear of death and his desire for honor. He fears death, but he also fears thinking about his fear of death. Perhaps he would take up such thoughts if there were someone like-minded in his outfit to offer emotional support for such thinking.

In this example, emotion does not threaten human rationality; it is the only possibility for engaging human rationality. It is emotion, the fear of death, that generates a thought never before entertained. In order to continue with this thought, Kikuchi must have the courage to feel. And this, apparently, is something he cannot do. Courage makes reasoning possible. To have courage, however, entails reorganizing a network of feelings. What a "nightmare" this would be. Kikuchi protects his initial thought from its reasonable implications. Its link to other thoughts must be contained by having it "frogmarched under heavy guard" across his mind. Here Farrell, like Bion, observes a point where a potential rational sequence of thoughts is forestalled by anxiety. Kikuchi illustrates an everyday example of the desire not to know.

Kikuchi could save his life if he could think. He could save his own life if he could follow up on the logical possibilities of his initial thought. But he lacks the emotional resources needed to allow this thought to unfold. Kenneth Dodge argues that "all information processing is emotional, in that emotion is the energy that drives, organizes, amplifies, and attenuates cognitive activity and in turn is the experience and expression of this activity" (1991, 159).

Charlotte Gilman Perkins describes how the desire not to know may reflect severely limiting, but widespread, cultural assumptions.

In Gilman's short story "The Yellow Wallpaper," the heroine has been forced by her physician husband to confine herself in her room to "rest." While confined she thinks:

> If a physician of high standing, and one's own husband, assures friends and relatives that there is really nothing the matter with one but temporary nervous depression—a slight hysterical tendency—what is one to do? (Gilman [1892] 2002, 3)

These thoughts ask a question that suggests further possibilities for thought. What is one to do?

In this example we can see Gilman, the writer, observing the mind of her character much as Wilfred Bion observes the mind of her patients. The woman of the story is thinking about a problem. He husband claims there is "really nothing" the matter with her. And she struggles with this thought. She feels very much that something is wrong. She asks a question that opens up various possibilities for an answer. She asks, "What can one do?"

As many readers of Gilman now understand, there are many things you can do. You can question the premise of your husband's authority. Is one's husband, though a "physician of high standing," in fact, fully knowledgeable of the situation? When Gilman's character asked this question at the time of the story's publication, very few women could take such a step "forward."

Gilman's character initiates a series of thoughts that lead in a direction of questioning an authority, but it does not develop further thoughts for this heroine. Some force acts like a lid to control, deny, and suppress the productive activity of thinking. This force I am calling the desire not to know. At the time, Gilman's story was an immense puzzle for many readers who could think no further than the story's heroine. Now, though, it is easy to see how Gilman's short story, as a literary artifact, encouraged exactly the kind of thinking that the character is unable to do. The story now serves as a rallying cry for feminists who feel a need to question the authority of men. Gilman, as an early feminist, developed a discourse that made it easier for women to have the courage and capacity for honest self-reflection. When groups of women gathered together to give each other emotional support for the courage to think, the world changed for women.

The desire not to know reflects the workings of emotion. But the solution to the desire not to know is not to banish emotion from the context of thought but to explore and reflect upon the various demands of emotion in relation to any context of thought. The exploration of emotion can work as a reorganization of emotion, and this reorganization allows the core self to broaden its conscious awareness and thus more effectively assimilate information for problem-solving purposes.

Reason, Emotion, and Experience in the Liberal Arts Classroom

Human action requires a smart assessment of objects, people, and goals. Aristotle observed that those who are "angry with the right person, to the right degree, at the right time, for the right purpose, and the right way are at an advantage" (*Nicomachean Ethics Book IV,* 5). Emotions define the logic for action. The work of finding the proper relation between our emotions and the condition of the world is a work of emotional development.

Liberal arts education has as its subject, records of human experience that communicate the emotional and affective quality of life. Novels, music, painting, dance express affective experience and courses in these fields invite students to take in these experiences and reflect upon and respond to them. The information of these affective records is often emotionally uncomfortable. But both the formal nature of art and the conditions of its study allow this information to be assimilated. Martha Nussbaum argues that liberal arts education can connect "experiences of vulnerability and surprise to curiosity and wonder, rather than to anxiety" (2010, 101).

There has been a persistent belief in Western culture that emotional experiences—and particularly formal practices that reflect upon emotional experience and integrate disparate and conflicting feeling states—have a unique capacity to "grow" a mind. These experiences have been traditionally associated with artistic expression and reception and with the liberal arts training in the humanities.

Ramachandran suggests that a good dose of cold water injected at the right time in human ears might solve many problems. This is not practical, but there are realistic responses to denial that do not involve injections of cold water. I will propose a spectrum of practices that work as pedagogical equivalents to Ramachandran's adjusting contextual beliefs and REM triggering.

A literal understanding of this research suggests that human beings can "dream" their way into new relations with new information. I am not in a position to claim that students who take courses reading authors such as Toni Morrison and William Faulkner take in new, uncomfortable information and then dream their way into the integration of such information. I suspect that this may indeed happen. Certainly it would be useful to research such a possibility. Dreaming may indeed be the path to what Seigel terms the "reorganization of existing memory traces."

We do not have basic information on the role of dreaming in learning. Prior to the new work in neuroscience, no one would fund such research. We do, however, know something about the role of processes very similar to dreaming in their work upon emotional reorganization and information assimilation. The newly emerging field of neuroaesthetics suggests that aesthetic experience contributes to memory consolidation, and more importantly, to more flexible styles of information exploration (Kafka 2012).

Liberal arts courses typically examine human experience, ask questions about its meaning, explore affective experience, encourage interpersonal discussion, allow for sustained affect examination, and often revise existing feelings. Liberal arts courses typically engage the emotional lives of their students and seek to actively promote an emotional synthesis of thought.

Reflection has emerged as a useful concept for understanding emotional reorganizations in the assimilation of information. Reflection defines a practice where conscious thought doubles back on itself to consider its own content. The effect of such a practice can be to redefine frameworks that, initially frozen and controlling, become suspect or modified as the mind achieves agency over an otherwise passive event. Reflection is particularly important for the arts. Beth Thomas describes "meaning making" as a practice of "conscious reflection" (2012, 334). Reflection often has an unacknowledged emotional component. Through reflection, emotions not yet fully entertained can be brought into active contemplation. Through active contemplation, new feelings are produced by contemplating old feelings in a new context. These new feelings can be then be brought to bear upon understanding. New feelings toward information thus allow the assimilation of information. This dimension of reflection requires time, and time becomes another key factor in the emotional assimilation of thought. The brain will fully experience different emotional contexts only at different moments in time.

Ken Bain's highly influential book on teaching *What the Best College Teachers Do*, observes that good teaching has a personal quality that adjusts to the immediacy of the student's emotional life. "Teaching is not acting," he says. Good teachers do expect to affect their audience when they talk: to capture their attention, to inspire, to provoke thoughts and questions. Good teachers learn how to adjust to their learning of needs of their students. They "define" and "mold" their ambitions, Bain says, "in a process that is both rational and emotional. This practice has all the power of careful analysis, but it also entails the energy of feelings and attitudes that no induction and deduction can achieve (2004, 121).

Good teaching helps students take in new information. It uses reason, but it also responds to emotional cues of student responses. It adjusts the impact of the message to the emotional and nervous system of the learner. Bain points out:

> Most of the teachers we studied frequently used rhetorical questions, even if it was no more than to ask, "Does his make sense?" They watched their students' reactions, read their eyes and other body language, and adjusted what they said to the enlightened, confused, bewildered, or even bored looks they saw in the classroom. (Bain 2004, 118)

As educators, we should not simply hope that such processes take place. We can more directly promote processes of emotional integration.

Classroom silence is one quality of student engagement that good teachers learn to read. Inexperienced teachers are often uncomfortable with silence. Silence often means that the teacher does not know what students are thinking. Silence can sometimes be hostile. But some forms of silence express deep reflection. Teachers can teach students to honor such moments and value what products arise from reflective thought.

Reverie is perhaps more powerful than reflection in the dream work of learning. Reverie is different from reflection insofar as the conscious mind fades back from center stage to allow memories and daydreams to become involuntarily entertained. In reverie, as in dreaming, emotions that cannot be retrieved at will or by reflection can emerge spontaneously for reflective consideration. Eric Kandel, a Nobel Prize winner known for his work on the biology of memory, now pioneers a field termed "neuroasethetics" that seeks to document the importance of art and reverie for human development. Alexander Kafka, writing for the *Chronicle of Higher Education*, represents his work thus:

> Art isn't, as Kandel paraphrases a concept from the late philosopher of art Denis Dutton, "a byproduct of evolution, but rather an evolutionary adaptation—an instinctual trait—that helps us survive because it is crucial to our well-being." The arts encode information, stories, and perspectives that allow us to appraise courses of action and the feelings and motives of others in a palatable, low-risk way. Sometimes instinctively, sometimes more consciously, artists play with perception's variables in keen acknowledgment of the viewer's active role. (2012)

Reverie is not discussed extensively in educational literature. But it is an experienced dimension of human engagement. Good teachers instinctively know how to promote reflection and reverie. Good teachers know the importance of these processes and sense these activities in the silences that attend classroom discussions. Ken Bain describes the actions of the good teachers he researched:

> Robert Divine knows how to ask a good question in the seminar and then how to wait patiently, even through several minutes of silence, while his students thought about their answers. Sometimes highly effective lecturers will pause ever so slightly following a key point and stand perfectly still; their body language will suggest suspended animation as they work to keep their students attention focused on the point and to give them time to contemplate it. They know how to make silence loud. (2004, 120)

As universities shift more and more to online learning and large classrooms, teaching of the kind done by Robert Divine is less available. Practices that make effective use of reflection and reverie are replaced by practices that distribute facts and use impersonal lectures to impart impersonal knowledge.

What we lose is not just particular instances of effective teaching, but a finely crafted social practice that has been honed by years of direct classroom experience. Good teaching teaches students not just how to make use of some information; it teaches students attitudes for learning information. They develop skills from Divine's courses that they can bring to bear on other tasks. As the problems of information assimilation become more dramatically clear, we should become more aware of our responsibilities as educators.

Summary

The argument of this book is first that college and universities must not only produce information but also help students assimilate information. The assimilation of information I describe requires an engagement with the emotional lives of students. This emotional attention is not in any form a "therapy," but it does require attention to emotional experience. Traditional teaching in the liberal arts offers this practice. Many successful teachers already follow the suggestions I recommend in this book. Many administrators, however, see no value in these practices. The understanding of reason and emotion offered to us by many researchers in neuroscience may persuade administrators of the importance of emotion to thought. In addition, careful attention to the relations between reason and emotion can make all teachers better teachers.

In the four chapters that follow I will offer selected examples of the desire not to know as I have observed it and offer some initial principles for the emotional assimilation of knowledge. Chapter two offers a closely observed, particular example of classroom experience. Chapter three offers a broad outline of the emotional dialectics of thought, a dynamic that shifts between highly rigid and highly permeable moments of human interaction and information assimilation. Chapter four argues that traditional academic training, particularly training in the liberal arts, does not prepare professors for the skills they need to be effective in recognizing the emotional ground of thought. Chapter five examines the current state of academia where online courses increasingly replace face-to-face courses. This form of education, highly popular among administrators, may threaten, but perhaps enhance, many of the most useful practices of the liberal arts classroom.

Just as Bion's psychoanalytic practice placed emphasis on doing emotional work to recover freedom for the possibilities of thought, my book describes a practice of teaching that gives attention to the negotiations of emotional context that often go unacknowledged in academic discussions. Laughter and humor is a particularly important component in classroom discussions. Just as speakers may seek to "loosen up" their audience with a joke, so also teachers can respond to anxiety in the classroom with a joke, or more subtly, respond to laughter in the classroom with an observation that generates anxiety. The emotional give and take of classroom interaction is in fact the generative ground of thought. Teachers who try to force thoughts upon students through sheer insistence, demand, and intimidation most often generate merely more anxiety to generate more complex and effective defensive thoughts. Laugher, humor, anxiety, and interest have been given plentiful scholarly attention, but this attention lacks the subtle discriminations that can systematically evaluate how these emotions contribute to or hinder the assimilation of uncomfortable thought.

Because teachers, by talking face to face with their students, can engage their emotions and explore the emotional contexts of discussion across a wide range of themes when they detect anxiety and opposition, teaching can shift a desire not to know into a curiosity-to-know. This working with the emotional context of thought resembles in some respects the work done with emotions in therapy, but this classroom work is not therapy. It is not a form of group therapy and it does not ask students to reveal their personal lives. Students are not asked to change their values nor look into their libidinal histories. Instead both students and teachers are asked to observe how memory and the linking relations of developing of thought can be deflected by anxiety, shame, or pride. Students and teachers are asked to look at how patterns of anxiety or laughter developing in the classroom may direct or dismiss the generation of thought.

In a classroom, thought emerges dramatically from the emotional interactions among students and teachers. Most often this interaction is an accident of unconscious forces that clash and merge in interpersonal interaction. By thoughtful attention this drama of interaction can be made more, rather than less, productive for integrative thought. Psychiatrist Daniel Siegel argues that "educators can benefit from insights into how emotion and interpersonal relationships are fundamental motivational aspects of learning and memory" (1999, xii). This book outlines principles for the emotional assimilation of knowledge. Such a practice grows the mind's capacity to be thoughtful, reflective, and adaptive to new information.

When we see resistance or defensiveness in other people, we often "recognize" it as a kind of moral failure. It is more useful to think of it as bumping up against the biological limits of thought. If we are really serious about working with information assimilation, we must recognize the real biological limits of thought and work with the processes of thought that are effective for brain functions. While it may be true that different people exhibit different degrees of limitation, it will be helpful to not blame people for their limits. These limits are not chosen, they are effects of a history the individual had little capacity to control.

Notes

1. The concept "resistance" can imply a Marxist framework describing ideological rigidity. The term can also be used in a psychoanalytic framework that gestures toward concepts such as denial, disavowal, and projective defense. These frames are commonly used by scholars in the humanities. A great deal of work has been done in the humanities on the concept of resistance in the classroom. Much current literature in educational theory describes the difficulties in learning new information in political terms. The concept of "resistance," for example, is often employed to describe students' failure to take in repudiated knowledge. Students thus are resistant because they have political attachments. Henry Giroux's *Theory and Resistance in Education*, for example, endorses a radical pedagogy that emphasizes the "reifications of daily life." Giroux's goal is to bring students to understand how all knowledge is a "product of social relations." Giroux's analysis, like the work done by composition scholar James Berlin, gives central attention to political ideological structures that are dominant in everyday discourse. This work is a useful theoretical account of knowledge and social relations. But more work needs to be done to understand how social relations have emotional dimensions, grounded in body experiences of shame, contempt, anxiety, and fear.

    Shoshana Felman (1989) discusses resistance in psychoanalytic terms making use of Lacan's phrase, "passion for ignorance." This is a helpful addition to political accounts of resistance that derive primarily from theories of ideology. But Lacan's insistence on our "passion for ignorance" does not help us understand how to work with this passion when we encounter it in the classroom. Lynn Worsham's 1998 article "Going Postal: Pedagogic Violence and the Schooling of Emotion" is often credited as an important beginning for a more serious consideration of emotion in the classroom, contributing to something that has been called "Critical Emotion Studies." Affect and emotion, Worsham argued, determine how the world of language, the symbolic, takes hold and binds the subject to a set of feelings, thoughts, and relations. Three particularly useful books have recently been published in this field: *Doing Emotion: Rhetoric, Writing, Teaching* by Laura Micciche, *A Way to Move: Rhetorics of Emotion & Composition Studies* by Dale Jacobs and Laura Micciche, and *Teaching the Rhetoric of Resistance: The Popular Holocaust and Social Change in a Post 9/11 World* by Robert Samuels.

My book is most compatible with the work of my friend, Robert Samuels. I am seeking in my manuscript, on the one hand, to avoid Samuel's psychoanalytic vocabulary and use work in neuroscience and simple description to support claims made by Samuels, Bracher and myself in earlier work. On the other hand, I hope to offer a more sharply honed focus on the process that has been termed "resistance." My focus suggests that it not helpful to imagine resistance as an apparently bullheaded student. We simply become bullheaded teachers. It is more helpful to understand and work with the emotional processes that allow information processes to be effective.

2. This book will shift between two perspectives upon the failure to take in information. One perspective is that provided by contemporary neuroscience. The other perspective is one offered by clinical work that takes an empirical view of thought processes. Both of these views are incomplete. Careful work in sciences does not afford the easy generalizations that I am formulating in this book. I am using science for what I hope is intelligently informed stories about mental processes. I am taking the risk to speculate because I have come to believe there is a story to be told in this material.

Chapter Two
The Psychology and Biology of the Desire Not to Know

Many teachers wish to involve their students in debates over political issues. They know these discussions can be volatile and embattled. They do not want to insist on the superiority of their own beliefs. But they do want to make claims of fact connect to a rational process of thought that can motivate responsible political action.

In these situations, teachers often feel divided between two equally undesirable options. On the one hand, they can supply information and not worry about how students use it. On the other hand, they can do more than supply information; they can also pressure students in various ways to use information as they themselves wish. In the first instance they run the risk of being ineffective and in the second instance they run the risk of being authoritarian.

I propose a method of teaching that recognizes that the simple supply of information most often has little impact upon fixated styles of thought. This perspective recognizes that university teaching must take responsibility for what I am terming the emotional assimilation of information. This perspective does not, however, seek to put emotional pressure on students to think in particular ways. It works instead to bring into the sphere of thought an awareness of a range of emotional contexts that makes thought meaningful. This process appeals not to political truth but to a common desire for a greater freedom of thought in solving problems.

Too often teachers recognize the failure of rational thought, but feel powerless to do anything about it. This is a dilemma for teachers who seek to be both political and democratic. Our democratic principles make us reluctant to intrude into the personal values of our students. But our concern for global issues gives us worry. If we do not put some pressure upon irrational student belief, we are not really doing our job as teachers. Some scholars who sense the emotional complexity of thought advocate using emotional forces of various kinds to put pressure upon students. Students are seduced, intimidated, or confronted. I am suspicious of these procedures in their general tendency to force students through a process of thought that they do not experience as their own.

We must develop a mode of research and inquiry responsible to the emotional complexity of thought. The principles I propose do not employ emotional force to seduce or intimidate students. It does ask students to be reflective about how emotional experiences can reduce the rational possibilities of thought. In this chapter I will pay particular attention to three affects commonly observed in the classroom—anxiety, anger, and laughter. Anytime there is an abrupt shift in the subject and anytime there is a marked emotional response, the teacher seeks to track her class's anxiety to find ways to verbalize and reflect upon this affect.

There is a complex of other feelings and emotions often linked to my selected emotions—anxiety, anger, and laughter. These other feelings and emotions—pride, fear, shame, and disgust—are important. But I do not propose that we make a classroom a therapy session. We should not be asking our students to confess their secrets or compete with each other in expressive achievement. We need not ask students about their personal lives. We should, however, observe the emotions that develop in classroom discussion and talk about how these emotions facilitate and hinder thought. In my classes I find that laughter and contempt often legitimate a dismissal of new ideas and perspectives without discussion. If I am gentle with my response, I can suggest that contempt is effective in combating some ideas, but dismissal legitimated only by contempt is a refusal of the work of thought. Whenever emotion works to dismiss an invitation to thought, we must follow through with reflection. What other possible emotions might explore possibilities for thought?

My argument throughout is that emotion makes certain possible linkages in thought possible or impossible. The last ten years have seen a significant increase in interest in relations between thinking and emotion. Damasio, in *Descartes Error: Emotion, Reason, and the Human Brain,* explains that emotion can interfere with our ability to remember information. When memory is not available for reflection, rational thought is sabotaged. Whenever we speculate upon what is good for us or for others, we are necessarily and legitimately in conversation with years of emotional history and memory. The good will always be meaningful in relation to remembered feelings. We do some of this remembering consciously, but, as Damasio explains, most of these experiences must be unconscious in order for the brain to operate efficiently. Joseph LeDoux's *The Emotional Brain: The Mysterious Underpinnings of Emotional Life* explores the complex links between consciousness and unconscious emotion, paying particular attention to memories of anxiety and fear. Anxiety and fear are vitality effects we feel deep in our bodies; they are markers for what is not good. For this reason our "thoughts" of what is "not good" are most often not effects of reason, but deep, visceral experiences rooted in primitive and tenaciously assertive memories still dominant in brain systems not flexibly responsive to prefrontal lobe thinking. Daniel Siegel describes emotion as a "value signal for the appraisal of meaning." All information from the external world, he points out, is not equally welcome. We have immediate emotional responses to the information that is presented to us. Unconsciously, by means of our "instinctive" emotional feelings, we evaluate the information we receive (Siegel 1999, 136). "Value systems in the brain function by way of increasing states of arousal" (137). Most of us can sense the emotional implications of a developing line of thought. If we sense the discomfort implicit in a potential thought, our minds will go elsewhere. As emotion determines the development of thought, the simple supply of crucial information often has little impact upon fixated patterns of thought and established habits of behavior.

In response to this failure in the simple supply of information, I propose that teachers do more to examine and negotiate emotion as it emerges and interacts with thought in classroom discussion. By "negotiate emotion" I do not mean "attempt to control emotional responses." A social group ideal for thinking is alert to any pressure of manipulation and insists upon the experience of an individual freedom of thought. This commitment, though, puts significant pressure on the teacher. If you are truly committed to freedom of thought, if you are in principle seeking to support freedom of thought, you must demonstrate your own ability to tolerate anxiety when your beliefs are threatened. If you place this demand on yourself, you will find that it is in fact very difficult to do. It is hard, but it is not an impossible goal to strive toward.

I have observed two significant challenges to this principle of freedom of expression. One challenge takes place when teachers cannot give up their need to assert their opinions. I see this style of thinking as totalitarian. A different challenge takes place when teachers are so charismatic that students idealize them fervently. In these cases students are so eager to think whatever the teacher thinks, that they sacrifice whatever emotional conflicts they experience in relation to the teacher's claims. There is very little conflict in such teaching. Whatever conflict might exist from students more firmly in touch with their memories and feelings is never explored.

I propose a teaching that brings into the domain of reflection characteristic emotions that indicate a "desire not to know." In seeking awareness of these emotions, I appeal to an ideal most of us share, a desire for a greater freedom of thought.

Rhetoricians from Aristotle to Fish have pointed out that new information does not reliably produce the assimilation of such information. In some situations there is an immediate and effective assimilation of information. When radio traffic reporters give information to motorists about tie-ups, they report that they can immediately see cars turning off major roads to avoid congestion. In this case information enters effortlessly into a reasoning process and human beings make changes in their behavior.

In other situations, however, a gap separates new information from a reasoning process that would produce change. People are often, and for various reasons, resistant to take in information that, though it solves real practical problems, conflicts with their identities and their key values. Under such conditions people deny the truth or accommodate it through suffering and sacrifice. They do not abandon beliefs called into question by factual information; they resist modes of reasoning that threaten their identities. A classic literary example of this is reflected in *Antigone* when the soldier responsible for guarding the body of Polynices fears to tell Creon the news that the body has been given funeral rites. Although the guard has done his duty well, he fears that Creon, in his anger at hearing information he does not want to hear, will kill the man who delivers the information.

In contemporary politics a constant battle seems to wage between leaders who insist upon the value of their policies and reporters who ask political leaders to recognize factual truths that contradict political claims. This problem is a wound to democracy and a problem that educators should address. And yet it has been a tricky problem to address because, like the problem it describes, knowledge of the problem threatens identities and cherished beliefs.

Terry Eagleton, in *Ideology: An Introduction*, points out that when Hitler needed more manpower for his military efforts, he continued to use in noncombat position soldiers to guard, police, and exterminate Jewish people. Though his first priority, according to reason, should have been to win the war, he refused to release men to important combat locations because he was committed to a policy that, in addition to being criminally insane, had no military importance. Hitler's actions were self-destructive. He could have freed up much-needed manpower. He could even have used Jewish prisoners in various sectors of his army, but he refused such thinking as if it were a personal contamination.

Hitler's desire not to think contributed to his loss. Current leaders, our own leaders, repeat patterns of thought similar to those I have described in Creon and Hitler. Present political leaders dismiss, obfuscate, and fail to acknowledge factual information in order to pursue ideologically correct policies. Information from the intelligence community and from the scientific community is dismissed and misrepresented.

The desire not to know is perhaps the greatest threat to democratic values and practices that we face. It produces costly mistakes at the level of national decisions, it produces costly mistakes in terms of personal decisions, and it generates dangerous conflicts between peoples. Although some attention is given to the emotional lives of students in college curriculums, no curriculum and no discipline systematically examine and make us of the links between emotion and reason. In earlier times, education was linked to emotional growth. In 1921, shortly after the enormous pain and destruction of World War I, the British Newbold Report proposed that England should teach English literature in an attempt to "humanize" people and provide much needed values for a world gravely wounded by war. Much of the Newbold Report appeals to religious models for value, but nonetheless the intention of the report was to develop human sensibility through the study of art. I am not proposing that we use the Newbold Report to formulate educational policy change. But I do suggest that we take seriously an idea that has had credibility in the past. Our educational system must take the emotional lives of students into serious consideration.

If university courses work more carefully with the emotional ground of thought, they can contribute to more flexible minds, minds better able to make use of new information. Teachers usually imagine that they teach students who want to learn. Often students do want to learn; sometimes they don't. Students bring to the classroom a rich and diverse array of prior experiences, values, thoughts, ideas, and cherished beliefs. Teachers teach their subject, but most of them understand that what they teach can conflict with what students want to believe.

How can we respond to this challenge of teaching something that is repudiated? Are there methods for working more productively with the resistances and with the possibilities for dialogue that emerge in this situation? I will begin a discussion of this question by making use of a psychological perspective on the desire not to know as it was formulated by Wilfred Bion. In chapter one I used work from neurobiology to explain how an understanding of the brain can help us understand the enormous resistance to thought that teachers frequently encounter. In this chapter I will make use of Bion's concept to observe how new ideas generate a complex set of emotional responses that serve the desire not to know.

Bion's ([1962a] 1977, [1962b] 1984) concept of minus K (–K) is much discussed in therapeutic research as "desire not to know." Bion developed his theory of –K in an attempt to make sense of situations where a patient in analysis does not want to know the thoughts that are beginning to form in his own mind. As one rule of analysis is "free association," clinicians can follow a developing line of thought as patients speak their moment-by-moment thought.

In response to this not-yet conscious movement toward thought, a patient can experience what Bion called an unconscious "attack on linking." This "attack" on the next step of thought is a "motivated" but generally unconscious movement away from the unease that a developing thought generates. This attack, thus, undoes the linking of thoughts that are in some process of formation.

What is useful for teachers is Bion's attention to a mind in a struggle with itself. There is a movement toward knowing. There is an emergent knowledge working itself toward consciousness. This transfer of knowledge takes place not from one person to another person, but from one sector of the self that desires to know to a different sector of the self that desire not to know.

Ramachandran's anosognosia patients are useful to keep in mind for understanding the importance of emotion for thought production. Patients who could not observe the loss of control of their arm under normal conditions, could observe the loss of control if they believed that the loss of control was due to an injection of a temporary paralyzing agent. When Damasio argues that memory is dependent upon "the emotional implications of memory," his generalizations suggest that thought, to the extent that it draws upon memory, will also be curtailed by "emotional implications." Thus a rational pattern for thought can move forward in a visible manner, only to become lost as a variety of anxieties take mental representations elsewhere. The emergence of knowledge depends not on an acceptance of verbal claims but on the emotional contexts facilitating thought.

Bion's –K: An Extended Example

Bion gave careful attention to instances when the mind does not want to take in knowledge that is, in an unformulated way, already "contained" by it. In such a case knowledge is "present" but is not fully "formulated" (that is working within accessible memory) as an acceptable verbal understanding. Though an emergent linking of unformulated thought could produce useful thought, –K undoes the linking that would form this recognition. Going back to the example from J. G. Farrell, we could surmise that a Japanese soldier, Kikuchi, joins the Imperial army with the intention to do his duty and serve with honor. Under combat conditions, however, he has a more clear understanding of what it means to follow orders and risk his life. The emotion of fear, linked to his mind's need to solve problems, begins to generate the thought that his commander is foolhardy. This thought begins with an emotional prompt that is generated by a facial observation—Kikuchi feeling uneasy when looking into the eyes of his commanding officer:

> Every time he met those burning eyes it was as if he received an electric shock. The intensity of feeling in Matsusita, his utter devotion to the emperor and to his country... Yet there was something that Kikuchi found rather frightening... Sometimes it almost

seemed as if he wanted to get not only himself but everyone else killed too.

The thought had crossed Kikuchi's mind—indeed it had to be frogmarched across his mind under heavy guard and swiftly, like a deserter who must not be allowed to contaminate his fellows. (Farrell 1973, 371)

Kikuchi cautiously manages to think. It "almost seemed," Farrell says, describing a thought that can almost be thought, but remains still at some distance from the initial glimmer of awareness. The full thought almost recognized here is that perhaps his commanding officer is so devoted to glory in warfare that he wants to get himself and everyone else (and thus the thinker Kikuchi) killed. This thought teeters on full countenance, but it threatens Kikuchi so much that it has to be carefully contained. It is "heavily guarded" and "frogmarched" so that it has no potential to link up with other thoughts. There is a danger here that the emerging thought, "might get everyone killed," might get linked to another thought, "might get me killed," and linked, further, to another thought, "if I want to save my life I had better disobey or dessert."

As a therapist Bion saw many examples such as this and formulated a term to explain how the mind responds to an uncomfortable thought. K, for Bion, represented knowledge. The mind, as it spontaneously responds to problems that need solutions, wants to know. Bion suggested that the dynamic of k operates as both a + k and a − k, suggesting that at times we are very curious to know things and at other times we have no desire at all to know things.

Minus k is not an easy concept to explain. Bion's terms have a mathematical austerity similar to Lacan's (1972) mathemes. Bion sought to describe thought processes in terms of algebraic representations such as "L," "H," "K," and" −K." It is easy to fill in each of Bion's letters with an equivalent conceptual representation. L, H, and K stand for the terms love, hate, and knowledge. And he suggests that "thought" is most often generated by emotion rather than by reason. What is particularly helpful in Bion's analysis of thought is its immediate practicality. Bion argued that links in thought most often follow links in emotional association. People often think about what they love and avoid what they hate, although they may think about what they hate, perhaps even obsessively. But, of course, they do not think about this hated object with the free flexibility of logical reason; their representations of it are hateful representations; chains of thought elements are generated and linked by the associational logic of hatred. Everyday illustrations are found in expressions such as "Love is blind" and "The first casualty of war is the truth." Students will often talk emphatically about what they "love" and "hate" in class discussion. I find that what is important in these claims is how they either open up discussion or close it down.

If a student says, in reference to the novel I am teaching, something like "I hate *Heart of Darkness*," it may mean that they really cannot enjoy thinking about it anymore. I must concede that there is very little I can do. The most practical thing is to accept what the student says and indicate to her that I understand and even sympathize with this condition. I too sometimes find myself in situations where I hate something and can't stand to think about it anymore.

Sometimes though, the sentence "I hate *Heart of Darkness*" is a kind of initial joking gambit to see what I, the teacher, will say in return. When I sense this I will ask a student what they hate about it, and if there is anything they like in it.

Bion's emphasis that thought comes from the emotions "L" and "H" can be useful in reminding us that the representations that we have in our minds derive often from core emotions, love and hate. Love and hate generate and direct thought, connecting people to objects, ideas, and other people, or the reverse.

If a student says she hates *Heart of Darkness*, what I need to think about is not simply the text, but the emotional context of the student's mind. Can I negotiate this hate through an appeal to other feelings? Are there generalizations I can make that will resituate the emotional dynamics of the student's thought? Can I ask the student to reflect upon her feelings so that the initial response of discomfort shifts? Can I direct attention from what is discomforting in the text to something in the text that arouses curiosity? Can I engage this student with other students who feel differently so that the student takes an interest in another's interest?

Clinical experience provides a context that allows therapists to observe carefully how people form and avoid links in thought. Very often therapy does its most useful work in relation to things that people do not want to talk about. Usually, when people do not want to talk about things it is because thinking about these things makes them anxious. Hence they do not think about these things.

But anytime thought is rejected, intelligent action is also rejected. Uncomfortable situations that cannot be thought can slowly become more badly managed and turn into intolerable situations.

Bion developed his concepts from analytic experience and over the course of many books and papers (*Learning from Experience*, 1962; *Elements of Psychoanalysis*, 1963; *Transformations*, 1965) he developed concepts and examples of his observations. I offer some of these examples later in this chapter, but I will say in advance that Bion's claims are often much like those of Lacan; they are rhetorically powerful in their appeal to our imagination, but they are not always conceptually clear. Readers are often frustrated by attempts to make systematic sense of Bion's pithy sentences.

To introduce Bion's concept of the desire not to know, I begin with a nonclinical example, which, for me, is at once obvious and usefully complex. In his response to the widespread approbation of Joseph Conrad's *Heart of Darkness* (1899) in American universities, Chinua Achebe ([1977] 2001) argues that the basic structure of Conrad's text reflects a desire not to know Africa. Achebe's account of Conrad's genius was directly antithetical to the then vast body of criticism that idealized the apparently sublime profundity of Conrad's literary achievement. Thirty years ago most scholars did not want to take Achebe seriously. Now Achebe's reading of Conrad is widely accepted, widely anthologized, and theoretically central to literary study. I confess that 30 years ago I myself published an essay on Conrad and did not want to accept or even think about Achebe's analysis of Conrad's novella. Now, however, I find his analysis sobering and useful.

Achebe was never trained in clinical "close observation" but he had developed a novelist's ability to see patterns of thought. His analysis of Conrad's mind cut through entrenched literary idealizations to reveal a disturbing quality in Conrad's avowed desire, as he stated in his "An Informal Preface", to "awaken in the hearts of the beholders that feeling of unavoidable solidarity... which binds men to each other and all mankind to the visible universe" (Conrad [1891] 1988, 225).

"In Western psychology," Achebe says, "there is a desire to set up Africa as a foil to Europe, a place of negations both remote and vaguely familiar, in comparison with which Europe's own state of spiritual grace will be manifest" ([1977] 2001, 1784). Achebe points to repeated patterns in the novel where sharp binary oppositions of black-white, civilized-savage, developed-primitive, moral-amoral contrast the world of the West with the world of Africa. Achebe calls attention to the setting of the narrative as a framework for simplistic binary thinking: "The book opens on the river Thames, tranquil, resting, peacefully" (1785) but soon opens up onto a scene of another world, dark and savage with both a sinister silence and a threatening intonation of drums. What he is describing is a curiously resonant geographical space. In the literal sense, this place is Africa, but most readers of Conrad understand this imagined geography as the space of the mind. One area of this space is, as Conrad says, "tranquil, resting, and peaceful," and the other area is the opposite. It is the uncivilized inner self, a savage world of sinister silence and savage drums that is awakened by the real country, which, for Conrad, is uncivilized, violent, and outside morality.

The novella, moving back and forth between what is seen and what is not seen, becomes, Achebe argues, a record of a restless struggle against a repudiated knowledge. Conrad wrote, "The earth seemed unearthly... It was unearthly and the men were... No they were not human" ([1899] 1988, 106). And later Conrad wrote, "Yes it was ugly enough but if you were man enough you would admit to yourself that there was in you just the faintest trace of a response to the terrible frankness of that noise... What thrilled you was just the thought of their humanity—like yours... Ugly (106).

There are many powerful images, philosophical allusions, and rhetorical resonances in *Heart of Darkness,* but the ideological drive of the text, Achebe says, is determined by a single clear desire, the desire to represent the world as one clearly divided along East-West and black-white lines. One world is white, good, sane, and civilized; the other world is black, barbaric, sinister, and uncivilized. For one who insists on seeing the world this way, complex sets of objects and observations become fodder for an implacable purpose. A powerful linking of object to object aligns the "thought" of the novel—not to know Africa and Africans and to avoid knowing it and them.

Achebe's analysis of Conrad as a writer with a desire not to know usefully illustrates a few points important for teaching. It suggests that in many cases the desire not to know to know is staged as an unfinished dialectic. Desiring not to know becomes caught in the movements of fascination that pull the thinker toward knowing, and there are thoughts that register this emerging recognition. Later, however, fearful thoughts push an emerging recognition away from the thinker.

Therapists see patients avoiding emergent thought all the time as they "work" with the oscillating waves of anxiety that often accompany thinking. Therapists seek to create, or at times wait for, propitious moments and contexts for the linking action necessary for an emerging thought. Just as the thinking that takes place in clinical experience often follows an alternating seesaw course between moments of denial and moments of insight, so also can Conrad's novella be understood as a struggle between moments of uncomfortable and minimal acceptance. Sometimes, Conrad seems to acknowledge a kinship with Africans, and at other times he forcefully repudiates such knowledge. This struggle is part of the rhythm of many sentences in his book.

At some points the novel seems to express something like a physical disgust for a continent and its inhabitants. Conrad seems very fearful of some reality just outside the scope of his imagination: midnight ceremonies, African mistresses, expressive dancing, and drumming. This reality that Conrad fears is one that his central character, Kurtz, knows well, but (according to the narrative) this knowledge is obtained at the price of the loss of sanity. Conrad is fascinated with Kurtz and his knowing. He wants to know what Kurtz knows. But he situates Kurtz as someone who has morally fallen off the face of the earth. And thus he concludes that some desires for knowledge are better abandoned.

Kurtz, we learn, had something like a nervous breakdown. His nerves, Conrad says, "went wrong" and "caused him to preside at certain midnight dances ending with unspeakable rites" ([1899] 1988, 121). These midnight ceremonies, with their unspeakable rites, seem to represent thought possibilities "going wrong." They are possibilities for thought toward which Conrad is drawn but that he fundamentally abhors.

I believe that Conrad's text is not unique in its back-and-forth movement between wishing to know and wishing not to know. *Heart of Darkness,* like much other literature, represents the dialectic of a struggle between a certain fascination to know and a particular dread of knowing. I believe also that art is often just such an embattled expression. It may well be that, when we introduce into the classroom contemporary novels that address controversial issues, we are staging for our students a dialectic between knowing and not knowing much like Conrad's.

The Desire Not to Know in the Classroom

A good deal of what we teach in the humanities is important as well as difficult because it concerns knowledge that is ideologically suspicious and therefore repudiated or held at arm's length. We teachers in the humanities often must push against the conceptual limits of our students' moral comfort. At times this work can be fun for both us and our students. Students can come to college eager to be liberated from a more constraining world. And then our work can be much appreciated. When students "identify" with us, they may happily think our thoughts. But under many circumstances students do not identify with us. They hear our thoughts, spoken to them as sentences, but they do not think these thoughts. In such situations, students are not at all eager to take in new ideas. Our work is difficult, fraught with tension, anxiety, bitterness, and repudiation.

Some professors sense anxiety in the classrooms and respond. Other professors seem oblivious of it. Geoffrey Harpham, head of the National Humanities Center, writes about giving a talk on the humanities at The University of Damascus in Syria. When he hears the Muslim call for prayer outside his auditorium, he pauses for a moment to consider what differences there might be between his own assumptions about the humanities and the assumptions of his audience. He observes:

> As noncontroversial as these points were to me, I felt a certain risk in making them, conscious that my audience might have been offended at the obviousness of my presentation. But as I spoke, I imagined that they were not offended. In fact, through the myriad ways a silent audience can communicate with a lecturer, my listeners seemed to me to be particularly focused, almost as if they found the argument interesting. (Harpham 2010, 6)

Harpham's mind is actively alert, not only to his subject matter, but also to the "myriad ways a silent audience can communicate with a lecturer." Harpham does not explicitly describe how this information is conveyed. And in fact, his mental attention to his audience is also linked to his attention to his own inner thoughts, which focus on a few words—the "humanities," the "self." Harpham's observation demonstrates how a good teacher often looks to his students for cues to understand where to slow down a presentation and how to unpack particular terms that generate offence or resistance. Harpham's narrative indicates that teachers often work productively with these principles—but often tacitly and implicitly rather than consciously.

Harpham's report of his awareness of the mood of his audience is an important testimony regarding how good teachers and good speakers operate. They do not simply read fully finished papers. They do not insist upon the truth of their own reality. They sense the mood of their audience and adjust their words, to avoid insult at some points, and stimulate curiosity at other points. Good teachers do this, but very little effort is made to teach less successful teachers to learn these skills. There is no generally accepted pedagogical framework for thinking about the emotional lives of students. We do not readily grasp that emotion is connected to an ability to think. In literary theory and composition theory affect theory has become a term for people exploring the role of emotion in human action and expression. But much suspicion still surrounds this methodology. Many scholars are committed to what Jenny Edbauer describes in her own work as a "persistent critique" of affect scholarship. Christina Albrecth-Crane, responding to complaints from Edbauer and others, acknowledges that most affect theory is so theoretical that it becomes impossible to apply to the classroom. Additionally, many scholars are committed to a principle of pure rationality, fearing that any attention to emotion will quickly become indulgent, chaotic, and maudlin.

Ken Bain's description of what good teachers do suggests that teachers attentive to affect teach better. When teachers sense anxiety in the classroom they often seek a way to address it, to bring the anxiety into discussion so that it can be managed. Unacknowledged anxiety often shifts into anger and at that point there are few possibilities to challenge students to think.

Bion's concept of the desire not to know is a term from clinical practice, but it does not posit some theoretical concept remote from the practice of everyday observation. Most of us observe moments in conversation when friends or colleagues become uncomfortable with a subject. We sense that they are uncomfortable. To use the words of my students we "don't go there." Perhaps I should use the jargon of my students rather than the jargon of Bion for the key term of his book. But I choose Bion over contemporary jargon because, first, it offers a broad umbrella for understanding student resistance. Second, it offers linked concepts that inform us how to observe and think about this event with more intelligence.

I will use Achebe's account of Conrad's desire not to know as my first sustained example of a non-Western thinker simply being smart in observing how another mind works. Achebe offers a detailed observation of a mind (Joseph Conrad's) approaching but then backing away from a developing thought. Conrad, as Achebe reads him (and I agree), moves toward recognitions that he becomes increasingly uncomfortable with.

We can better understand how to challenge students if we better understand Achebe's account of Conrad. Conrad encountered experiences in the real world that pushed him to recognize what he does not, in fact, want to accept: that Africans are humans like him. He recognizes this truth in some part of his mind, but this recognition is very uncomfortable for him. His struggle to think is a struggle within himself. If a teacher were to try to step in to help give birth to this emerging but repudiated thought, she would, like an analyst, have to be very attentive to the periodic waves of anxiety that accompany this repudiated thought. She would have to be attentive to contexts that diminish anxiety, and she would have to work on the emergence of this thought under those conditions.

Conrad wrestles with this thought, admits to it at moments, but then works desperately to make it go away. He makes the thought go away, not by refusing to think, but by having other thoughts that take his thinking elsewhere. He generates thoughts that carry a strong emotional response and thus move his thinking to other locations and meanings. Minus k, in this example, is not, then, a simple avoidance of thought. There is a great deal of thought in the book. It is simply that these thoughts are generated precisely to avoid a real thought that threatens to emerge and disturb an ideologically idealized sense of self.

Recognition of thinking that avoids thought is important for teachers who teach repudiated knowledge. Sentences that contain "thoughts" are very protean forms of energy. Thoughts can begin anywhere and go anywhere. In the work of thought, very much can be done; ideation can be linked to neuronal links and to bodily activity. But ideation can also go around in elaborate circles of complex signification that accomplish nothing. Thinking that "goes elsewhere" can at times be useful for reducing anxiety, but it can also be used as a defense.

Stating a sentence that represents a thought that a teacher wants to teach does not, by itself, do the work of thinking. Stating a sentence repeatedly does not encourage a student to take in the thought of the sentence. Thinking is work. But the work of thought is not like driving a nail into a piece of lumber. The work of thought is in the complex resituating of the thought over time in various remembered emotional frameworks so that a propitious synthesis of linked meanings can make the emergent thought possible and alive with meaning.

This complex resituating of thought in new contexts where different emotional attitudes allow reflective cognitive consolidation is part of the creative work of teaching. There is no substitute for it. You cannot drive a thought into the mind of a thinker. You must allow and encourage minds to do their own proper work of contextual assimilation. Changing contexts for thought can allow an anxious thought to become drained of its attendant anxiety.

Achebe offers a carefully observed description of the anxiety that supports Conrad's -K. Conrad's avoidance of thought is clear, detailed, and self-evident. At this time in history, Achebe's analysis is an obvious account of a desire not to know as it operates in literary narrative. I have emphasized the dialectical movement of Conrad's narrative, but I want to give particular attention to two points before I turn to examine classroom experience. First, the truth that Conrad is avoiding is not something forced on him from outside. It is not, as is too often the case with teaching, that someone in the external world is claiming a truth that the thinker resists. Rather, it is that the thinker himself has generated this thought and is preoccupied with the particular dynamics of his own internal struggle.

Let me make a second, very different point. Conrad's unformulated thought is very much an internal and private issue of the mind. But Conrad's failed recognition of his own thought has wider political implications. What is at stake in the defense against a thought is not simply the personal experience or emotional growth of a writer, reader, or student. Not thinking a thought about the equality of Africa and Africans has clear political implications for a wider social world. Conrad's desire not to know his own thought has clear political implications. The teaching of *Heart of Darkness* and other works as either a knowing or not knowing has clear political implications.

I believe that teachers in the humanities do their most important work in largely unconscious ways, especially when they generate discussions that help students think a progressive writer's thought. Classrooms offer complex contexts for thinking. Teacher and students in dialogue generate talk that shifts about within a complex of emotional contexts. The mood of the class can shift from laughter to contempt and back to laughter again. Teachers and students constantly seek ways to allow or impede the emergence of unfamiliar thoughts. Some classrooms become places where students look forward to thinking and talking, yet some classrooms become sites of oppression. In either case, it is in the complex emotional recontextualizations of thought that teachers can find or produce contexts that can allow unfamiliar thoughts to become registered.

Achebe's analysis of Conrad leads me to examine how the struggle not to know can become staged within a dialectical process that embraces moments of knowing later elided by moments of avoidance. The dialectic suggests to me some hope for thought. In contrast to Achebe's claims, Conrad's struggle not to know may have led to some small progress in knowing. Even at a time when Africans were seen as less than human, Conrad worried that perhaps their humanity was not so different from our own. His struggle to repress was not altogether successful. I think this failure to repress completely gives us a clue to how to work with repudiated material. The dialectical struggle to think an unthought thought shows potential when there is a back-and-forth movement across the boundaries of fear and fascination. The teacher's task is to know how to make use of the two poles between which the thought vacillates. Neither pole is responsive to force. The fascination pole offers possibilities for useful curiosity but seldom for rigorous focused thought. The fear pole needs to be respected as a place where possibilities for thought have decisively shut down.

We all have experienced situations when conflicts in thinking became quickly volatile. They take us by surprise and make classrooms uncomfortable paces. Heidi Burgess (2009), codirector of the

University of Colorado Conflict Research Consortium, observes, "On occasion, teachers and students may find themselves involved in highly emotional discussions in the classroom. Sometimes these situations are unexpected: a student will accuse the teacher or another student of a racial or discriminatory remark or action, someone will get angry about a political comment, or someone will be upset about a policy or a grade." I began this chapter with the claim that three particularly important emotions for the teacher to observe are anxiety, anger, and laughter. This post by Burgess suggests that teachers commonly notice anger in the classroom.

I believe that when conflict over different claims about knowing arises in a context of surprised and overt confrontation, the desire not to know quickly becomes rigid. The mind responds to anger as an attack much as the body responds to physical attack. Possibilities for a dialectical engagement with undesired thought become minimal. I offer an extended example of this in an account of a scholarly presentation in chapter four.

In situations such as this, thought is not a tool for solving problems, but a weapon for defense or attack. Debate reaffirms established positions and repudiates dialectical possibilities. Debates rarely offer moments for sustained and vulnerable reflection.

I am particularly interested in classroom situations that sense the sites of conflict and open up dialectical operations exactly at those sites. Conrad's oscillating relationship between desiring to know and desiring not to know offers a useful framework for thinking about the classroom in this way. If we add Bion's account of -K in clinical experience to Achebe's analysis of Conrad's desire not to know, we can more carefully grasp the conditions that allow the emergence of dialectical possibilities for thought.

Thinking as a Problem-Solving Activity

Bion argued that, ideally, thought emerges as an adaptive, almost instinctive attempt to solve real problems in the real world. After reading Derrida and Lacan for almost 20 years, I find claims like that helpful. Thinking is something the mind is led to do because we live in a world that poses problems to be solved. Much of the time we make choices without having to think about the nature of thought itself—how to get snow off our sidewalks, how to clean pots. or how to get to various destinations. We desire an object, recognize its distance from us; thought comes to us, and our body turns a steering wheel or picks up a snow shovel. In contexts such as these, we need not worry abstractly about the nature of thought. Thought is present to us and we modify our actions according to its promptings.

Bion gave emphasis to important relations between thought and frustration. Thought begins when we cannot have what we want. The banana is outside our grasp, so our thoughts become tools to extend our reach. It thus makes sense, in a limited way, to think of thought as a tool. If thoughts were only tools, though, thinking would be easier than it is.

For Bion thoughts were often internal objects that we may seek or avoid. In this case we are not agents using the objects as tools; instead, our thoughts are determined by already existing relations between words and feeling (Bion [1962b] 1984). Words that resonate discomfort cannot call forth thought. Bion argued that "incapacity for tolerating frustration tips the scales in the direction of the evasion of frustration... What should be a thought... instead becomes a bad object... fit only for evacuation" (Bion [1962b] 1984, 307). What we call "thought" is, in fact, a linking of mental representation. The final effect of this linking is not thought but the avoidance of thought, the evacuation of a bad object. What seems to be thought generates ideation that leads us to know the world less and promotes conditions where we cannot solve problems that need to be solved. The ideation we term thought is attached to representations whose purpose is to defend against the emergence of problem-solving thought. In this case, what we call thinking is a clever avoidance of thought. With respect to Conrad's *Heart of Darkness,* we may even idealize as profundity something that is really the avoidance of thought.

Bion's reference to thought content as a "bad object" needing to be evacuated introduces an important claim regarding the relation between thought and internal objects. Thoughts are clearly present as internal representations, a kind of "object" (if I use that term stripped of its clinical jargon). But it would be a mistake to think of thoughts as mere signifiers to be effortlessly subjected to the process of reason. Signifiers can be manipulated through easy, logical manipulations. Internal objects are not so easily manipulated.

Numbers, for example, can be effortlessly manipulated by reason. Objects are not so easily manipulated. We do not "think" our relation to our internal objects. When we are young, our parents are "internal representations" for us. We experience their presence, but we do not control how we feel when we experience their presence. We seldom "represent" our parents with full flexibility of rational thought. We characteristically have strong feeling about our parents. We love or hate our parents and it is our emotions that determine what kinds of thoughts we will have. And we usually have different feelings in different contexts of memory. Thought, in these cases, has little freedom because it is constrained by the already existing circumstances of our emotional relations.

When we are the accidents of our affective relations to other people, our thoughts are determined by these affects. Bion emphasized love and hate as the affects that influence our thoughts. Let me give Bion's observations more emphasis. Mere signifiers yield to our logical manipulations of them. Thoughts tied to internal representations remain emotionally alive. They are "objects" that appear in our minds. They resist the effortless, logical manipulations of thought. These internal objects impose on us constraints on the production of thought. Strong parent objects forbid certain thoughts; strong cultural objects demand thoughts that are in congruence with their patterns of idealization. We dare not think thoughts critical of a beloved parent or fatherland.

John Lenzi argues that "ignorance, love, and hate have traditionally been recognized as the basic triad of human passions" (2006, 170). Lenzi summarizes the work of Bion to suggest that ignorance develops in relation to the child's earliest experiences of relationship: "Bion elaborated a psychoanalytic theory of thinking to explain how the ability to think develops in infancy... He constructed his theory of thinking out of the unconscious dynamics of Love, Hate, and Knowledge, or his shorthand L. H. and K" (170). The infant, Bion suggests, begins not with thought, but with relationship. Relationship here means hating, loving, and, the third category, desiring to know, which is a mode of relating that is not entirely dominated by loving and hating. Lenzi argues that initially "K was not an abstract mental function" but "an emotional function linking two people" (171).

Bion ([1962a] 1977, [1962b] 1984, 1963, 1965) invites us to appreciate that knowing must emerge very cautiously from the primary feeling states. People are loved and hated, and so also are objects of thought loved and hated. There are thoughts we fall in love with and thoughts we walk away from. Surely this is obvious. Much political response is based on loving and hating. And this is a problem. When a woman in Nebraska argues that Barack Obama is an African-born Muslim who wants to undermine American values, she is not, in the literal sense of the word, thinking. She is expressing the accident of her emotional relation to objects. And it would be a mistake to respond to her claims with thought, as if her productions as a thought could be brought into some discipline by someone else's thought. Thought will not move her, because her words are doing the work of relating, not of thinking. She is, like Ramachandran's patient with anosognosia, maintaining her own condition of safety. And it is regrettable that her verbal claims can have traction in an external world.

Our thoughts are often "objects" and our relation to them partakes of our relation to the object relations (in clinical terms) in our inner world. Our desire to know is in constant danger because it slides into the dynamics of love and hate that shut down thought and reduce it to emotional signifiers that express that love or hate. The desire to know, Bion ([1962a] 1977, [1962b] 1984) argued, characteristically works in relation to the desire to relate. Lenzi observes, "The developmental prototype of K was the intimate physical and psychological relationship between mother and infant. He formulates this relation as xKy. This means that x is in a state of getting to know y and y is in a state of becoming known by x" (2006, 171).

Much good thinking evolves from our relation to good thinkers: transference effects in relation to teachers, therapists, parents. New experiences in relation contribute to new experiences of thinking. Much of Bion's work explores how being in relation to a thought has much in common with being in relation to a person. Thoughts are often objects that elude us or visit us with attendant emotional effects. They bring us comfort or they bring us terror. Often, when we try to think about "what is true," we discover that "what is true" is experienced as an act of violence attacking that which we love. Thought, suffering directly from this violence, becomes restless and jumbled.

Bion's ([1962a] 1977, [1962b] 1984) analysis of the desire to know posits three possible steps that can be taken as the person moves forward toward knowing. First, a person can come to know something of the object. Second, in the development of a desire to know, a person's thinking can be undone by anxiety, frustration, hate, or love. In this case the movement to knowing is undone by −K, a desire not to know. There is also a third possibility. In cases of severe thought disorder, patients experience what Bion called a no K, a complete destruction of the capacity to think.

Bion outlined his observations of link-by-link developments of thought. He gave a number of complex examples to describe how in the struggle to think, a link-by-link relation of ideas can go astray at each step or even catastrophically. Here is an example of a catastrophic destruction of the linking process. Bion is describing the session as a representation of "the destructive attack on a link":

> Half the session passed in silence; the patient then announced that a piece of iron had fallen on the floor. [This was hallucinated.] Thereafter he made a series of convulsive movements in silence as if he felt he was being physically assaulted from within. I said he could not establish contact with me because of his fear of what was going on inside him. He confirmed this by saying that he felt he was being murdered. (1959, 309)

I suggested earlier that some "objects" of thought are experienced not as objects but as "acts" of violence. Bion's patient described in the passage physically reacted to the violence of his own thought when he made a "series of convulsive movements." We do not often see our students "convulse" in response to thought. But we do, I am afraid, witness the kind of silence that Bion observes in the first sentence.

There is something about the deadness in this silence that reminds me of the silence I encounter in some classes, both in my own and in classes I have visited as an evaluator. Students seem locked in an anxious silence. They feel under attack, perhaps even murdered. Their thinking is either deadened or in rebellion. I take this to be the dialectical end point of the desire not to know. We may, through discussion and through repeated statements that are experienced as a form of violence, bring our students to an end point where they are unable to tolerate the frustration of thinking. They come to hate a class or hate a teacher.

And here I have some questions. Can we recognize this place when we produce it? Can we understand how we produce it? Is there something we can do about this end point when we find ourselves here?

Stephen Patterson's blog report on one of his philosophy classes expresses a degree of emotional frustration I seldom see in published essays on pedagogy.

> This past term I had a rather unpleasant experience in my critical thinking class. I was confronted with a subset of students who walked in the door assured that I had nothing to teach them about critical thinking. I learned this because they vocally resisted absolutely everything with which they did not personally agree. Unfortunately, this wound up being nearly everything in the class—especially when it ran against the notion that everything is a matter of opinion, a matter for an eternal debate in which all views are equally right.
>
> Now, many readers are probably thinking, "cry me a river, that happens to me every term". I agree. It happens to me almost every term too. What was different this time was how long it lasted (all term, without let-up) and how deep the resistance went. (Patterson 2011)

Patterson recognized that his resistance was deeply emotional in nature. He says, "I got the distinct impression that my refrain that sometimes it takes more than an affirmative 'gut feeling' to make it reasonable to hold a position was being taken as a personal affront." Like many of us, Patterson wants to insist that students learn to use reason. That after all is what we, as teachers, are enjoined to teach. But if reason, as Damasio argues, must be linked to emotion, then teaching must find ways to work with students in exploring links between emotion and reason.

A clinician in therapeutic practice carefully observes the emotional tenor of a patient's mental activity. She learns to recognize moments of anxiety and reflection, and she learns how to introduce fearful thoughts in terms of small experiences of fear, rather than in terms of large, insistent, and repeated logical claims that generate more anxiety, fear or hostility. She learns to match moments of emotional openness to small possibilities for real thought about anxious subjects. Teachers who are effective in working with emotion, like good therapists, observe how other minds—the minds of their students—emotionally entertain possibilities for thought. Thought is not simply linguistic representation of abstract ideation; thought extends in subtle ways into the emotional physiology of the body that can be read in the emotional gestures of the face.

I will present a few real classroom examples that were attempts to read or anticipate the silence that Bion describes. These are examples of teachers who learned to "read" the silence and respond to it so that students could be emotionally "moved" from silence to dialectic. The first example is from a Russian colleague (Dmitryi Galkin) who was himself a student in a class that had reached the point I have described: there was general silence, resistance, and discomfort. This was a class in politics at the Russian University of Tomsk, where the professor was teaching Marx. The class was taking place just after the downfall of the Soviet system, and the students did not want to read or think about Marx. The professor could have continued teaching the silent class, or she could have made some response to the silence she encountered. She decided to respond to the silence. She asked the students about their discomfort. They were at first slow to say anything, but finally they told her that they felt that Marx was a dead thinker. They wanted to learn about Western non-Marxist ideas.

The teacher, who had taught Marx in the Soviet system with great discipline for many years, thought about this request. Finally she asked the students to read Hegel and a number of other thinkers, as a context for thinking about the contribution of Marx to Western philosophy. By shifting the attention of the class from Marx to Hegel, she was able to begin by focusing on something students wanted to know and only later return to teach Marx very successfully. Teachers, I think, do things like this often. They often know how to start thought at a place where students desire to know. By starting at this place, they can often bring students to desire to know what they do not want to know.

My Class on Marx

A second example of reading anxiety in the classroom comes from my own teaching. This particular experience convinced me that working with the desire not to know is much more than an event taking place in the minds of our students. It can become an intersubjective chess game of sorts in which the anxiety that attends thought—the anxiety that generates the desire not to know—is shifted from us to our students and then given back to us. If we continue to play the game, we shift this anxiety back to our students, who then may shift the same anxiety back to us until someone in this game finds a way to reduce its intensity through reflective integration.

Classes generate emotional contexts, such as shame and ridicule, that make nuanced thought difficult. In this way classes generate, spontaneously and without conscious intent, anxious moments for thinking. Class discussion becomes an ongoing group struggle with the anxiety attending thought. It constantly threatens to polarize the group and undo the work of thought. This chess game of anxiety, however, can be better managed if we, as teachers, become responsible for our own emotional role in the game.

I will relate three particular moments from my own classroom experience teaching Karl Marx. In choosing Marx, I am aware I will make many readers anxious. As of the time I am writing, January 2013, we live in a culture where many people believe that some systems of thought are dangerous. This fear of the danger of a system of thought, contributes, I believe, to failures in the assimilation of thought.

I will present two different but overlapping accounts of what happened in my classroom. In this first account I will give particular attention to moments of laughter as they interacted with the text I was teaching. The laughter is readily observable and memorable. For me, the exchange of jokes with my students is part of the joys of teaching. My first report on my teaching experience, then, will not probe deeply into the emotional life of the class. It will simply observe a particular emotional response, laughter, and explore the pattern of thinking and anxiety that the laughter marked. In my second report on the same experience I will be more reflective about the emotional substrate present but not fully visible in the first account. I seek to look deeper into the emotions that manipulated both my thinking and my students' thinking. My "depth" approach, however, will not be psychological but biological. When laughter has an edge of ridicule, we can begin to explore the biology of shame working in the repartees of social laughter. Shame, I will demonstrate later, has remarkable abilities to reduce possibilities for thought.

An easy way to generate hatred in a student is to shame him. Hatred and shame are not often seen in the classroom, but when these emotions are seen, it is usually too late to remedy the injury.

What we must do as teachers is to avoid the developing links that would produce these results. Laughter, because it can slide into ridicule, is an emotive response that requires careful observation.

Let me begin with the focus on laughter. Perhaps a good generalization about how the laughter in my class worked initially would be to say that this laughter functioned as social bonding. My class and I generated laughter as we worked together to assimilate and critique the ideas of Karl Marx. What I think I can show is that these responses of laughter worked first to accept Marxist appeals to "distribute wealth," but later to determinedly ridicule the idea of distributing wealth, and then, finally, to hesitantly explore and recognize the value of emotional self-reflection. I started out trying to teach Marx, but what I finally taught, I think, was the importance of reflecting upon how emotion can dissociate us from thought.

At the time that I went through this process I was myself, like most teachers, I assume, primarily focused on the subject matter of my teaching. I wanted to read a controversial text carefully: designate important concepts, summarize broad themes, and formulate clear sentences to represent this analysis. Marx was a radical thinker for his time. Some of his ideas are now commonly accepted, some are not.

I was teaching a course on interpretation as part of an advanced writing class at George Washington University. In setting up my syllabus I chose material that offered challenges in thought and interpretation. I had assigned stories by Conan Doyle, a novel on dreams, and texts by Freud and Marx. The day before I was scheduled to teach Marx's *Communist Manifesto*, I wanted to set up a context that would defuse some of the tension that I often encounter with the text. I do not seek to persuade students of particular points of view, but I do try to encourage students to entertain different points of view alien to their own. It has been my experience that controversial texts, like those of Freud and Marx, often become caught within the contexts of fixed belief systems. The beliefs express strong feelings that do not allow flexible thought.

Before I began class, I explored the web to see how other teachers represented Marx. I was looking for a way to suggest that many of Marx's then radical ideas are now accepted without question within the American system. I hoped that this approach would overcome some of the initial hostility that many students feel.

After a bit of research I located a website now linked to "Liberty Zone Café." At the time I was teaching, I found a web page that made the following argument:

> Americans, being the most naive people among the nations, now believe that Communism is dead because the Berlin Wall and the Iron Curtain have been removed. The ironic truth is that Communism has just switched names to become more "politically correct." Today it is called international democracy. The reason that the Berlin Wall came crashing down is not because Communism is dead but because they have achieved the planned agenda to communize the West, including America. Washington D.C. has indeed become part of the New World Order of atheist governments. With the last vestiges of Christian law having been removed from "American government" over the last twenty years, there is no longer a threat of resistance against world Communism. In reality, "American government" became part of the Iron Curtain, thus there was no more need for the likes of a Berlin Wall. Once again, in their foolishness, the American public has believed the lies of their "leaders" who applaud "the fall of Communism," while they have sold out the country to anti-Christian, anti-American statutes and regulations on the federal, state, and local levels. Posted below is a comparison of the original ten planks of the Communist Manifesto written by Karl Marx in 1848, along with the American adopted counterpart of each of the planks. The American people have truly been "buried in Communism" by their own politicians of both the Republican and Democratic parties. (Liberty Zone Café 2006)

I was amused by this argument and I thought that if I took this material to class the students would experience an initial amusement that would lead easily to a relaxed discussion and analysis. The argument would generate laughter and the laughter would help people relax in their response to some discomforting ideas. One quality that I genuinely admired about the web argument was that it read Marx's ten planks carefully. Additionally, it made a clear political argument out of a careful representation of Marx's claims. It quoted Marx word for word and sought to formulate broader logical generalizations on the basis of an exact representation.

A crucial line in the author's argument was the following point: "One other thing to remember, Karl Marx was stating in the Communist Manifesto that these planks will test whether a country has become communist or not. If they are all in effect and in force the country IS communist" (Liberty Zone Café 2006). After listing the ten planks, and showing how for each plank, the American government had set in place a form of government control roughly analogous to the reformations Marx sought, the author concluded that America had become a communist country.

Let me take a moment to point out an irony here. The web author, like many teachers, thought that he could supply correct information that would trigger an important political recognition. The writer of the web page hoped to awaken an apparently sleeping American public and prod them to recognize an important political truth: American has become a communist country. The writer believed that a sharply formulated representation of facts and clear expression of reason could expose the government of Republican George Bush as a communist government. I expected I could take this argument to my class, read it without comment, and produce hilarious laughter.

I went to my class the following day, confident and prepared. The class developed much as I expected. I simply read the argument made by the web author, tried to keep a straight face myself, and the class broke out into hilarious laughter. The information presented by that author, rather than changing the beliefs of my class, instantly generated great ridicule. It is interesting that I needed to make no effort in asking the class to pay careful attention to the claim. It is as if they somehow "smelled" something "rotten" in the argument.

In retrospect, I have come to feel that the classroom laughter operated as a powerful emotional context that made it possible for people initially suspicious of Marx to be more comfortable with my discussion. In the context of this laughter, Marx, compared to people in the Liberty Café, was more American than the purported "true Americans" of the Liberty Café.

At the time I simply took this experience for granted. I had the sense of another successful day at work. I would now give my experience more scrutiny. It is clear that my class did not, when presented with this argument, work through the argument detail by detail. Instead there was a very general global awareness that triggered, not a thoughtfulness about the argument and its details, but a very general expression of ridicule and dismissal.

The web message—simply because of the markers of identity staged in it—triggered an immediate recognition that was exactly the opposite of the recognition the author wanted. Before there was any possibility for reflective thought, certain words demanded certain feelings. And thus the logic of reason formulated by the writer of the web page was completely dismissed by a force of feeling.

Words that marked the identity of the writer, "international democracy" and "New World Order" (used with great contempt), in opposition to other words like "American people" made students immediately suspicious of whatever thinking the writer wanted to generate to change their identity. Our shared classroom experience was one of reading the author's argument and dismissing it with contempt, and really without serious thought. We were all brought together with considerable emotional force by the powerful force of dismissive laughter.

When I chose the argument from the Internet I was motivated by little more than a vague desire to offer something that would loosen up discussion and help focus attention on the specific language of Marx. I assumed, really without thinking about it, that the argument was so badly constructed that the effect of these ideas upon my class would only produce laughter. I was correct in this assumption that the argument would produce laughter. But the laughter that I produced, I soon learned, went deeper and had more effects than I realized.

The first day the class and I had, I would say, a "good time" in our discussion of the website. No one expressed any sympathy for the belief that America had become a communist government. We all laughed at the crazy ideas of the writer. I was able to show, I thought, that the writer was partly correct. America had in fact incorporated social reforms that were very much in line with Marxist thought. The ideas put forward by Marx at the time, I argued, seemed crazy, but many of them are now widely accepted as good social policy. Americans are divided on the principle of offering welfare to the poor. But this policy has been in place for over one hundred years, and it is at this time an American, not a communist, practice. There may be an interesting irony here. Wealth distribution is a communist idea. Americans do agree on wealth distribution through income tax, but even Republicans who support income tax are uncomfortable thinking of themselves as having Marxist ideas.

My class on that first day ended, I thought, in a very positive way. I encountered emphatic criticism of Marx's desire to abolish private property but I encountered no real resistance to thinking about Marx as an innovative social thinker. No one seemed offended by reading him carefully. In this respect, that class represented the kind of work I wanted my students to do—to recognize that initial feelings about a well-known subject should not constrain possibilities for thought. When the class ended I thought I had done this work well.

On the following class day a student was scheduled to read his response to Marx's text. As is my usual practice, I had encouraged my students to say whatever they thought. When I had discussed Marx on the previous day I sought to read the text with respect. I expressed suspicion for some ideas and admiration for others. I hoped to set up through my own example a pattern where opposing points of view about the text could be expressed. I wanted my students to feel free to express their ideas but I also wanted their responses to show serious thought. I urged them to develop a disciplined and careful attention to the text. My student's response paper gave me what I wanted in many ways.

My student, let us imagine that his name was "Ben," had written a spirited and inventive response to communist ideas. He quoted the text often and offered paraphrases of basic ideas. As he was reading his paper, the class grew warmer and warmer as he himself became increasingly sarcastic toward the *Manifesto*. Ben was obviously pleased with the response of the class and earnestly talked through his paper, enthusiastically reading a sentence like the following one: "Marx, in his utmost naivete expects that human beings will work like hell all day for a year and then at the end of the year take their hard earned cash and share it with other people, with strangers who have not worked at all. This idea, as anyone can imagine, is totally crazy." Before he finished reading his sentence, the entire class broke into a kind of uncontrolled and hilarious laughter.

Let me give emphasis to the obvious differences between thoughts caught in powerful emotional contexts and thoughts experienced privately in the mind. There is an experienced difference between a matter of fact statement—"Marx's ideas are ridiculous"—and the enormously powerful rhetorical effect of an entire class laughing at an idea as ridiculous.

If Ben had simply said, "Marx's ideas are ridiculous," this would have been a statement that could be subjected to critical thought. In relation to a matter of fact statement, students, generally speaking, have some freedom to think within the privacy of their minds. In generating a powerful social laughter of ridicule, however, Ben very much worked with the latent emotions of his classmates. He called back into play the context of Marxist suspicion that I had hoped to dismantle earlier. He encouraged them to think of Marx as so ridiculous that serious thought about him was an affront to common sense.

I was very much surprised by the enthusiasm of the laughter I heard. It implied, I thought, that most of my students agreed with Ben. The laughter also, it seemed to me, completely annihilated all that I had taught yesterday. Marx was no longer an innovative thinker located at an important moment in history. He was no longer linked to ideas that are (as the Liberty Zone Café argued) central to American assumptions about social justice. Marx was, instead, a dangerous lunatic.

I was uncomfortable during the laughter and conflicted in my response to it. For a good while I was angry, but unsure about what to say. My anger and conflicted feelings made it very difficult for me to think. When Ben finished reading, I was at first at a loss of words. Most of all I wanted to chastise my students for what I perceived as a lack of seriousness. I felt, however, that such an action would make them defensive and this would make it more difficult for me to generate a critical discussion.

After some silence, it occurred to me that I could simply ask my students to talk about what their laughter meant. What did the emotional release of their laughter mean in terms of what they thought about Marx? They were still feeling exuberant from having laughed so riotously, and were slow to shift gears in their thinking. Some of them simply had trouble making a shift from laughter to reflection and some of them perhaps sensed that I was not nearly as comfortable with the laughter as they were. I experienced a moment of uncomfortable silence in the classroom.

Now that I look back on it all, I think the uncomfortable silence I felt from my class was more uncomfortable for me than for them. They were, I think, generally feeling good—but having trouble thinking about my question. And as they labored to shift from laughing to thinking, I felt the oppressive weight of more silence. I did not at all feel good. I felt very much deflated by their laughter and I found it very difficult to imagine a useful response. It was, as if the riotous laughter had dismissed my authority as a teacher. I felt powerless in my ability to ask for serious thought.

Finally, I decided that I would simply say what I was thinking. I told them that I had the feeling that if I were to argue now that Marx's ideas were innovative contributions to social progress, most of them would dismiss the argument with more laughter. There was a general nodding of agreement and I sensed their interest in what I would say next. This first step of engagement with them restored my ability to think.

As I began to feel connected with them, I began to sort through my memories of previous classes in order to make sense of what had happened. It occurred to me to argue that what had happened in this response to Marx was an example of the operations of ideology that we had talked about the previous week. We had experienced the ideas of Marx as obviously totally crazy, as something not worth serious thought. But in fact, this idea that seemed totally foolish—that a person would want to contribute a part of his salary to other more needy people—was, as we had discussed the previous day, a key element of the American tax system.

And so what we had done today was, in a crazy way, to totally dismiss as ridiculous a basic American policy. We dismissed as ridiculous what in fact we do all the time in perfect good sense. This was an odd sort of observation. I suggested what "we" had just thought, with great satisfaction was, in a certain way "crazy." And this indicated, I argued, that things that are not crazy can seem very crazy in a particular emotional context.

My argument loosened up reflective thought. I had managed to make a shift from the exuberance of laughter to the curiosity of reflection. The class became alive and engaged again with thought and talk. I had asked them to think about the forces that deflected their ability to think, and they were interested in this line of analysis.

I pointed out that we had, the previous day, thought, as a group, that taxation to help the poor was a good thing. Today, however, a context of emotion had developed that led us to dismiss as totally crazy something that was, in fact, a part of basic American political policy. When I finished talking, there was another moment of laughter in the classroom. This laughter, unlike the laughter earlier, was not exuberant, but reflective.

My experience with laughter in the classroom represents something important about the emotional assimilation of information. I had led them to think about Marx on the first day of class, but my thinking did not help them assimilate the ideas of Marx. The thoughts I generated as a teacher on the first day of class were thoughtful but not "emotionally assimilated" into their long-term memory. These thoughts never became connected to their lived emotional life. The possibility for a deeper connection to the emotional life of thought emerged only when Ben triggered their real resistances to what I had taught on the first day. It was only when I asked them to think about the inconsistencies in their thought that they recognized and expressed an emotional response that worked upon the conflict between the two responses they had made. In responding emotionally to their first response by means of reflection, they began to make progress in the emotional work of assimilating thought.

I feel some confidence is suggesting that these three moments of laughter worked in roughly this way. On the first day the class laughed with me and at anti-Marxist ideas. I had used laughter as a context for ridicule that led them to think what I thought, but this thought had no real connection to their emotional thinking life. On the second day, urged by Ben, my class laughed at Marxist ideas and perhaps also at me to the extent that I was identified with these ideas, and thus used ridicule to undo the memories of the earlier class. Later on the second day my class laughed, though more soberly, at themselves. This laughter, I thought, was a reflective expression of their amusement at seeing the inconsistencies in their own thought.

As a teacher, I went through this experience without being very aware of how the expression and interaction of emotional responses provided a vital context for the act of thinking. I can now see that my teaching generated a complex set of emotions that situated possibilities for thought. Through our use of laughter we negotiated the power dynamics of our classroom interaction. One way to represent what had happened is this: I myself staged our thinking by using laughter, as a form of ridicule, to push my class to be contemptuous of simpleminded anti-Marxist thought. At the end of this class, I had a smug feeling of success. I had succeeded in bringing my class to laugh over the ridiculousness of anti-Marxist ideas on the first day. The success that I had the first day, however, seemed to have no real roots in the real emotional life of their thought. On the second day, a competent class leader used my own method, the laughter of ridicule, to push back against what I was urging them to think. They staged a social experience where I could either be part of their group by laughing with them at Marx, or I could stand alone and risk feeling the sting of their laughter as a ridiculing of my ideas. In this way, they put considerable pressure on me to laugh at Marx with them.

This experience taught me something important about the nature of thought. Engaged thinking works with emotion through a temporal horizon as various thoughts and feelings work through a variety of not yet experienced contradictions. It takes time for the various possibilities in the linkage of thought to develop. The more we seek to understand how emotional contexts provide impetus for linkages in thought, the more we may be able to give our students and ourselves the freedom to fully take up the critical work of thought.

That experience left me with weighty questions about teaching and the problems of working with the desire not to know. As a teacher, I had intuitively found a way to work with the resistance I expected from my students. If I had taught the Marx class for one day only, I would have felt very proud of my accomplishment. I would have felt that I had made progress in opening up their capacity for new forms of thinking. But when I gave my students the freedom to express their own thoughts, I found that they reverted to their habitual patterns of thinking. It was as if the work of my previous class had counted for nothing. As I write this book, this is not astonishing to me. But at the time it was. I had just taught an idea very effectively, but the very next class day, my students had no memory of the event.

Shame and the Biology of the Desire Not to Know

I narrated this story by giving attention only to emotions that can be easily observed. In this second section I will offer a more reflective account of my story. Having worked on this book, I am now in a better position to understand what happened in that class. Having worked on understanding relations between reason and emotion I can now better understand how emotion manipulated the work of reason I sought to promote.

The work of Eve Sedgwick and Sylvan Tomkins makes sense of the "desire not to know" from a biological perspective that highlights the sharp conflict between demands of thought and the demands of emotion. The biology of emotion in the body is often difficult to observe. Researchers argue that cultural experiences with shame and disgust set in place biological responses that restrict and attack possibilities for cognitive thought (Scheff 2000, Holodynski and Kronast 2009). Classroom experiences that appeal to demands for "thoughtfulness" should anticipate the biological ground of resistance and seek forms of engagement that address more than formal logic. When thought is forestalled by the demands of emotion, we must shift our attention to the emotional forces at work.

To address resistance, we must engage the logic of the emotion directly. Consider thought as an experience people have very similar to the experience of food. The internalization and emotional assimilation of thoughts has the same structure as the internalization of food. If one lives in a culture where some foods are viewed with disgust, there will be no headway in logical appeals that such food will do one good. Biological disgust responses immediately overrun possibilities for disinterested consideration. No thought about food will defeat the stronger disgust response with which the body has been trained. I may know for a fact that horse meat is "good food." But even if I know this, I cannot, by a confident appeal to my knowledge, induce you to eat a food your body recoils from.

My classroom narrative on teaching Marx reflects a process where, first, there is an "interest" in the development of thought, and later, an aversion to this very interest. This pattern is relatively common. It is as if people begin a line of thought that promises a solution to a problem, only to discover that the solution involves practices or thoughts that make them uncomfortable. They start out with ideas that are exciting, but they soon recognize, in the jargon of my present students, that they are happier if they "don't go there."

Bion assumes that people's minds work as responses to problems, but internal emotional conflicts can derail the development of potential thoughts. Thinking can make life better, but that does not mean the process of developing an initial thought into a solution to a problem is always successful. Many thoughts begin to develop but are undone by a process Bion calls an "attack on linking" (1959, [1962b] 1984). There is a struggle within a thinker between a desire, on the one hand, to work out the logical implications of a useful thought, and a desire, on the other hand, to avoid the anxiety or even pain that the expanding link to link complexity introduces.

Resistance is too often imagined as a struggle between two parties. The beliefs of a teacher conflict with the beliefs of a student. Bion complicates our all-too-common scenario of a resistance as a struggle of will between the minds of two opposed individuals—of a student determinedly resisting a teacher. He focuses instead on resistance as a struggle within a single mind. An interest in thinking is often in conflict with a resistance to thinking.

Bion describes the desire not to know as an attack on the following up on an interest. This description of resistance as a turning away from interest can be helpfully illustrated by a description of the biological impact of emotion on the body. In *Touching Feeling*, Eve Sedgwick opposes many principles of poststructuralist thought and much psychoanalytic thought, to give serious attention to the biology of emotion in the human body. Sedgwick observes that "shame, of all things, [is] what either enable[s] or disable[s] so basic a function as to be interested in the world" (2003, 97).

Sedgwick examines the role of affect in cultural productions and gives particular emphasis to the "near inescapable habits of thoughts that Foucault groups under the name of the repressive hypothesis" (2003). She is referring to a practice of binary thinking where two positions fight their way through a simple on/off form of logic that either attacks or defends a contested position. She describes this mode of critical engagement as being like two people sharing the same electric blanket. One wants the bed warmer, so she turns up the heat, but the other wants the bed cooler and so she turns down the heat. This struggle goes on without a solution. Sedgwick wants to encourage a more complex form of thinking that offers the sense of a dense interrelated texture for thought, an experience she describes as being similar to how touching offers the complex sensations of a multidimensional experience.

This opposition to binary thinking is helpful for understanding the emotional complexity of resistance. Binary responses to resistance are fruitless. We should seek possibilities for resistance in new forms of emotional engagement. Resistance implies a logic of opposition. But it is precisely this binary logic that undermines effective teaching.

Attentive to the embodied feel of emotion, Sedgwick examines how our emotions locate us within a lived world. Much of Sedgwick's thinking about affect comes from the work of Harvard psychologist Silvan Tomkins. Sedgwick published her own edited collection of writings from Tomkins in an edition titled *Shame and Its Sisters*. Shame is a key emotion for Sedgwick; she quotes Tomkins's observation that "like disgust, shame operates only after interest or enjoyment has been activated, and inhibits one or the other or both" (Sedgwick and Frank 1995, 5; Tomkins, 1963,123).

Tomkins's account of shame's disruption of interest has implications for the understanding shame in the classroom. A desire not to know can intrude when feelings of shame, linked to training in socially unacceptable thought, shut down the mind's need to explore the world. Shame disrupts the mind's movement to follow up on the logical implications of thought. We learn shame from other people and we often feel shame in response to social triggers. When shame is linked to disgust, biology shuts down possibilities for prefrontal thought and reflection.

Tomkins observes, "The shame response is an act which reduces facial communication" (1962, 119), suggesting that an ongoing bond between two people, teacher and student, for example, can be rudely broken by shame response. Shame thus not only inhibits interest, it disrupts and often wounds a social connection that would encourage interest.

Tomkins argues that shame "stands in the same relation to looking and smiling as silence stands to speech, and as disgust, nausea and vomiting stand to hunger and eating" (1963, 352). This insistence upon a close relation between shame and disgust calls attention to bodily experiences that are a felt component of emotion. Damasio argues that reason is linked to emotion. Tomkins reveals how cognitive experiences can have an unconscious and relatively instinctive biological form. A biological form limits possibilities for cognition. A thought linked to a disgust response is a disgusting thought. The emotion comes first and controls the experience of the thought.

When Tomkins suggests an analogy between a desire for social interaction and hunger, he gives attention to the analogy between taking in food and taking in thoughts from another. As omnivores, human beings (unlike many other animals who rely on relatively few food sources) must think about what they eat. They must decide what, out of the many choices for food, is their best choice. For most people these choices are made easier by cultural training. Each culture has its own food and taste preferences and most cultures have, in addition, highly effective food prohibitions.

Food prohibitions and thought prohibitions have a common ground. There is a biological pattern here that must operate in order for the body to survive. In conditions of hunger, a cognitive drive makes a demand upon the mind to look for food. This demand to look for food complements the biological drive of the body to eat. Under the body's drive of hunger, the mind's possibilities for thought are narrowed; the mind is slow to take up work other than looking for food. Hunger is a powerful force with particular aims that makes demands upon the mind to secure proper objects. The mind, responding to the prompts of the body, in the experience of hunger, looks for objects. It is acquisitive, explorative, and observant. Serving the biology of hunger, the mind experiences less freedom in the dynamics of thought.

The pressure of hunger must be important from a biological point of view because it is charged with the drive to keep the body alive. But though hunger is a powerful drive, there are equally powerful regulations placed upon the drive of hunger. Disgust, it seems, developed as a biological response providing humans with an almost "instinctive" protection again eating poisonous or rotten food. We might imagine a hungry early human foraging for food in a forest, coming across a dead rabbit, eager to eat the meat, but then instinctively rejecting it as the limbic system takes in the smell of rot. This instantaneous biological response to the smell of rot protects the biological organism from unfit or poisonous food. Disgust, then, like hunger, is a powerful drive expressing the needs of the body. And it also places limits upon the activity of the mind. We might go further and suggest that from a biological point of view hunger has to be a particularly powerful drive because its goal is to keep the body alive. But if disgust works, then it must be a drive more powerful than hunger. It immediately and abruptly restrains hunger from its acquisitive function.

Tomkins argues that disgust controls eating just as shame controls looking. This is helpful. Both hunger and looking are actions oriented toward taking objects into the body. Eating physically takes a food object into the body and looking psychologically takes a visual object into the mind. Both of these actions, however, are biologically regulated. Both shame and disgust make biological demands upon the body prompting actions that block the body from taking in an object that is not suitable, either not suitable for biological health, or, in effect, not suitable for psychological health.

An important biological feature of disgust is that if you feel nausea, you cannot easily eat, even if you think you should. If you do eat, you will have to force yourself to overcome a gag response that is part of the biological experience of disgust. If hunger is a biological force that stimulates a desire to eat, disgust is a biological force that stimulates a desire to not eat.

How then does thought fit into all this? What kind of force can thought have in relation to the biology of either shame or disgust? It would be foolish to imagine that the biological force of disgust can be rendered powerless, inert, and neutral by the logic of a rational thought.

What I am inviting you to imagine is that if student resistance is part of a disgust-shame dynamic, then asking a student to take in a "shameful" thought would be like asking a happy sophomore to eat a raw and rotting dead rat. There may be reasons why we would want a student to imagine that this practice is both easy and, at times, beneficial, but if we do not recognize that there is a disgust response in the body, our every attempt to persuade the student of the usefulness of the idea only repeats the disgust response that make the positive thought unimaginable. It is as if the teacher's action operates on two totally different levels of communication. At the verbal level, the teacher is asking a student to take in an idea. But this verbal level has no real presence for the student. The student is responding on a somatic level. The teacher's action demands that the student "swallow an object of disgust." The student feels outrage.

The teacher does not have a disgust response. And so she simply repeats the information he want conveyed. And she may repeat the idea over and over. But when she says, "Eating a raw, rotting, dead rat can be good," the student's limbic system responds only to the phrase "raw, rotting, dead rat," and there is a disgust response. The more we repeat the sentence with emphasis on the words "is good" in an attempt to convey knowledge, the more we trigger a biological disgust response to the words "raw dead rat." The resulting verbal interaction thus becomes a farce. The teacher tries to insist on knowledge, but simply reinforces the disgust response by the repetition of her very insistence to teach.

I am proposing that the biological ground of both shame and disgust responses help us to understand what Bion terms "the desire not to know." Bion describes the desire not to know as, at times, an attempt to "evacuate a bad object" ([1962b] 1984). Bion's term "bad object" reflects the vocabulary of object relations theory that describes that our inner representations of intimate relationships (parents, lovers, friends) as present to us as "internal objects." Both Freud and Klein argue that our earliest experiences of "taking in" images and relationships are modeled upon the intake of food. Freud (1913) speculated that a boy's identification works in terms of a fantasy of murdering and devouring his father. Later Freud (1915, 1917) uses the term "incorporation" to describe a primitive form of identification. Klein (1932) talks of relationships to the good or bad breasts as internalized objects within the self. This language of eating and parental bodies is off putting, but it signaled an understanding of thought similar to the understanding offered by Tomkins. Tomkins suggests that disgust, as a response to avoid an object of food, becomes the model for actions of thought. If an object is not fit for internalization, it is a "bad object," and thus an object that we desire not to know and desire not to hold in our minds for thought.

For Tomkins disgust is a biological response seeking to vomit out food content. Shame is a similar biological response. It stimulates a desire to not look, to not take in an image. Shame and disgust are related phenomena. Once disgust responses are established, we feel shame in inspecting that which is disgusting. And this implication goes further; shame stimulates a desire to not pay attention, to not think, to not follow up on thought itself. It is an often unconscious dynamic in Bion's description of "attacks on linking."

Disgust and nausea, Tomkins argues, are originally related to the biological experience of an instinctive refusal of taking in food. He theorizes that disgust is a "built in rejection mechanism specifically designed to enable the individual to avoid or eject food" (1962, 50). Vernon Kelly observes that "the actions of the head and face when disgust is triggered involve a forward movement of the head, a protrusion of the tongue, and a pushing down of the lower lip. If this response is very intense then vomiting occurs" (Primer of Affect Psychology, 18).

Evidence suggests that a large component of the disgust response is both universal and biological. Paul Ekman of the University of California, San Francisco, found that the facial response to disgust was identical in different cultures across the globe. People make this expression by turning up their noses and pulling down the corners of their mouths. Research also show that disgust may produce specific autonomic responses, such as reduced blood pressure, lowered heart rate, and decreased skin conductance along with changes in respiratory behavior. MRI scans also reveal that people use a special part of the brain when they are disgusted: the anterior insular cortex.

Late in the 1990s, Valerie Curtis at the London School of Hygiene and Tropical Medicine surveyed people in different countries to examine patterns in the disgust response. He found many responses very particular to certain cultures, but he also argued, on the basis of much shared biology, that there was a lot of overlap. Disgust is a common response to things that are unclean or inedible. Curtis speculated disgust could have been one of the first words uttered by humans. The word "yuck" is similar in languages all over the world.

Disgust may develop as a literal response to food, but it is clear that disgust responses now cover a wide range of reactions to things that are not tasted, smelled, or ingested. Just as food can be taken in or vomited out in disgust, so also a variety of beliefs or thoughts can be either taken in and metabolized (as they say in my institute) or vomited out in disgust. Furthermore the action described here is represented as, like the biology of disgust, an involuntary almost instinctive response. It is not as if one fully registers a thought and rejects it; it is more like the "smell" of a thought in the process of being formulated is expelled. Some kind of feeling coming into existence as thought is violently rejected.

Resistance Has a Biological Integrity That We Must Respect

If these arguments have validity, they suggest that what we see as resistance in our students can have a biological integrity that we must respect. We cannot expect to overcome a biological "gag" response by a logical argument. Such an assumption or practice is simply stupid.

I am reminded here of various pollution taboos connected with religious values. I remember my Hindu language teacher during my

India Peace Corps training sitting down next to me when I was eating meat. She looked over, about to say something, saw the food on my plate, and turned away looking a bit sick around the eyes. I would now interpret this as a disgust response. I was anticipating a pleasant conversation. But her response and my own response to her disgust response (laughter) made any conversation between us difficult for a long while.

Our two responses imply many things about the social and discursive effects of conflicting disgust responses. Her response in itself indicates the links between eating, thinking of eating, thinking and talking. She does not eat, but she clearly feels nauseous when looking at what I eat. It is her thought that produces her disgust, not her biological taking in of food. I felt uneasy with her response, but my "instinctive" manifest response to her gesture is laughter. My laughter protected my injured pride from a face that expressed disgust with my choice of food. But this laughter did not encourage thoughtful communication between us. It made communication between us uneasy for a considerable time. It wounded her further.

In the Hindu religion, as in most forms of religion, certain kinds of practices and thoughts are experienced as pollution. A high caste Hindu may need to wash her body if she touches food belonging to a low caste Hindu. Brahmins make need to bathe if they step in the shadow of an untouchable. Jews can feel sullied by nonkosher food. Muslims can feel defiled by the presence of pork. Christians may need to cleanse their souls if they have impure thoughts or indulge in impure practices. We could in fact generalize very widely in this manner. Many religions practice a variety of pollution taboos that restrict the kinds of things people can eat, touch, and think about.

I have described disgust responses as an effect of religious belief, but I am confident that the religious element here is a red herring. Any kind of social identification can and usually does involve assimilating a shame or disgust response, or both, to particular ideas or beliefs. It as if the social demands for psychological cleanliness become built upon innate disgust responses of the body. There is no "natural" disgust response to cooked meat. But with the proper training of children, such a response can be effectively taught. And the point of all this is that any real object and any item of thought can be effectively prohibited by social practice.

Work in sociology (Scheff and Retzinger 1991) argues that shame responses by a group are highly effective mechanisms for the social control of others. It is very difficult for people to think with a free range of thought when they are face to face with others who respond to their behavior with behavior that trains the body in proper shame or disgust responses.

Each social group formulates behavior that it treats as shameful. Unconscious anticipations of shame covertly keep people within acceptable social practices. Just as disgust polices the body laying down boundaries between inside and outside, clean and unclean, shame experiences lay down boundaries between us and them, between thinkable and unthinkable thoughts. Let me give an example from Peter Matthiessen's long novel, *Shadow Country*. The scene I am about to quote from involves a meeting between two kinsfolk. One of the characters, Lucius Watson, wants to learn more about his family history, but he discovers that asking questions leads to unbearable, I would say, "polluting" thoughts. Tomkins calls shame "an inhibitor of interest and enjoyment" (1963, 134) and a barrier to further exploration (1963, 135). This inhibition is clearly present in this vignette. In this scene Lucius is talking to his aunt about an incident from the past:

> Anxious to pursue his questions before a phone call from Lake City ended the interview, he asked how the family had reacted when Julian and Will were arrested as accessories after the fact in the Mike Tolen case and jailed on one thousand dollars bail. He assumed the family knew of this since it was on the record at the courthouse.
>
> Agitation entered the room like a wild bird through the window, thumping and fluttering behind the curtain. The ladies stared at him.
>
> *"Jailed?"* Ellie Collins drew herself up to stare him down; her baked expression seemed to say. *Is this how your repay me?* The family knew no such thing, she told him in a tone suggesting it could not be true and that, in grubbing through court documents, the self-styled "Professor" had indulged in unprofessional and dishonorable behavior. (Matthiessen 2008, 357)

Later this character, Lucius, is able to reflect:

> If the brothers had testified against an uncle of their blood, they had transgressed the oldest code of those Celtic ancestors who, despising

all authority, loyal only to the clan, had borne their tattered pennant of archaic honor across the seas into the New World. (Matthiessen 2008, 357)

This sentence informs us that Lucius has asked his aunt to think a polluting thought. The thought she is asked to think is factually true. But it is a thought that, for her, is unthinkable. The narrator tells us that "those Celtic ancestors" are fairly free of restrictive authorities; in fact they "despise" all authority. Nonetheless they carry situational rules that dictate what is polluting. A few pages later in the novel we are told that the unthinkablity of this thought is tied to its experience of shame.

The narrator says, "In the stillness of the old schoolhouse, he suffered with them the weight of shame inflicted on this family by Papa" (Matthiessen 2008, 358).

The Biology of Disgust Supports the Desire Not to Know

The work of Tomkins encourages us to consider resistance as part of a complex biological and cognitive process whereby the human embodied organism does not take in material that is experienced as poisonous. We normally think of thought as forms of representation managed easily by rational processes. It often seems as if we can logically manipulate all the representations of thought just as we can add numbers in math. The disgust description offered by Tomkins should encourage us to see cognition as having layers of affect, some of which are deeply intertwined with drive behavior and unresponsive to manipulations of conscious thought.

I have offered a lengthy discussion of shame and disgust because I believe that these emotions were emotional energies present but not quite visible in my interactions with my George Washington University class on Marx. I knew from experience that many of my students would find my teaching uncomfortable. I was looking for a way to throw the distrust that I expected off guard. When I ran across the Liberty Zone Café claims about Bush's government, I was amused and felt intuitively that this material would make my teaching easier.

I anticipated discomfort in my students and I used a position statement written by an ultra right wing that I had found on the Internet to operate as a foil to their own bias. My thinking about what I was doing could be represented thus. The Liberty Zone statement was very funny. I enjoyed reading it and I thought my students would enjoy it also. They did. My first class ended with me thinking that I had taught something.

What I did not think about then, was how laughter can express ridicule and organize groups by shared shame responses. We all laughed at the argument of the Liberty Zone Café, but our laughter was powerfully motivated by shared emotions that went unrecognized. The Liberty Zone Café expressed their contempt for Marx, but their most emphatic message was their disdain for the US government. This contempt and the radical generalizations that supported it, carried my students into a position in opposition to them. When I laughed at the "Ten Planks" argument, my students were eager to join me.

This made it easy for me to invite my students to feel sympathy for Marxist ideas. My laughter strategy was like Ramachandran injecting his anosognosia patients with a saline solution to change their feelings about their paralysis. When they think their arm is temporarily paralyzed, they can observe its inability to function. So also, at a moment when my students feel intense contempt for the intellectual deficiencies in anti-Marxists, they can also entertain some generally accepted versions of Marxist ideas.

Without knowing it, I set into play a dialectic of shame and contempt. When I asked the class to read this argument, I invited them to express ridicule toward it. They were happy to do so. As we all laughed together at some "Other," we bonded together and isolated outside of us an object of ridicule—the unknown writers of the web essay. The writers of the web essay, being fervent anti-Marxists, made it difficult, I think, for anyone in class who might have intense negative feelings about Marx to express themselves. The ridicule I invited my class to express, made its anti-Marxist's arguments difficult.

Looking back on it now, I wonder if anybody in class felt that the laughter, directed at radical anti-Marxists, felt the ridicule of that laughter was potentially directed at them. Did any of them feel the sting of ridicule in the laughter? Perhaps a few students secretly wanted to defend this denunciation of the Bush government. Perhaps I introduced a shame rage dynamic into the classroom with what I thought at the time was a harmless joke. This thought never occurred to me at the time, but it does give me pause for thought now. My point is that it is what we do unconsciously to organize the emotional tone of a class that most often determines the real possibilities of thought. It is more our emotional tone and emotional engagement than what we say in direct logical and conscious verbal assertion.

Most people in the class were suspicious of Marxist thought, but they conceded in the first class that America had need for a more equal distribution of wealth. It was beneficial to use some tax money to improve education and stimulate economic development in oppressed areas. These ideas were an important contribution to American political practice. These ideas were perhaps Marxist ideas initially, but they had become American ideas.

I felt very good about all this. I arrived at my next class on the *Manifesto* with contented confidence. When Ben read his report on the *Manifesto* and proceeded to argue that each idea was wildly absurd, he released whatever unexpressed reservations about Marx that my students did not find a space to express in the first class. I had thought that I had dismissed these ideas in my last class. But I had not. The contempt toward Marx that I had wanted to expunge on the first day came back on the second day in an intensified form. I had led this class to think Marxist ideas, but I had not helped them to emotionally assimilate these ideas.

My student used ridicule, much as I had. But in this case the ridicule was directed emphatically at Marxists and I think also at me. Ben spoke with a proud and sure expression of contempt: "Marx, in his complete failure to understand human nature, wants people to share their money with other people" My entire class seemed greatly taken with this gleeful power of ridicule.

I struggled between feelings of irritation and curiosity. Although I did not think it at the time, in retrospect I think I must have feared that I was myself the real object of my students' ridicule. They were directing their laughter and ridicule directly at Marx, but this laughter had created an intensely polarized social space. I felt that I was given the choice to either laugh with them or be the object of their ridicule. If I did not laugh with them I would identify myself as having an attachment to Marxist beliefs. In an effective but totally spontaneous manner my student was using my emotions to manipulate my ability to think, just as I had unwittingly done to him perhaps in the previous class.

In this second retelling of my story I will give more attention to the emotions I felt when I faced my class after my student's respond to the *Manifesto*. I said earlier that I had felt uncomfortable. I can now understand my response as Tomkins's shame response. I could not follow up on my own interests. It was difficult to meet my students' smiling faces with a shared smile. I had trouble remembering what I had been thinking earlier.

I was uncomfortable during the laughter and conflicted in my response to it. For a good while I was angry, but unsure about what to say. I very strongly had the sense that I needed to be able to remember what had happened in class earlier. But I found that though I tried hard, my memory of my previous class was failing me. When my student finished reading, I was at a loss for words. I wanted to chastise the class for not being serious. I felt, however, that if I showed irritation, it would make them defensive and this would make it more difficult for me to generate a critical discussion.

I faced my students with what I hope may have been patient silence. I had the sense that if this silence lasted too long it would itself become a kind of crisis. They would read my silence as either anger or embarrassment. I found this silence painful, but after awhile, it occurred to me that I could simply ask them to talk about what their laughter meant. When this idea came to me I felt great relief. Looking back on it now I think it was crucial that I responded to their shaming response with interest. When I took interest in their thinking, even though it threatened me, they were able to take interest again in my thinking. Slowly and hesitantly we began to repair the social bonds that the laughter had unraveled.

I asked them what their laughter meant as "thought." They were still feeling good with the experience of laughter, and they were slow to respond to my question. Some of them simply had trouble making a shift from laughter to speech, and some of them sensed that I was not nearly as comfortable with the laughter as they were. I experienced at this point a second moment of uncomfortable silence. My first moment of silence came in my response to their laughter and the second moment came in their silence in response to my question.

Looking back on it now, I think the uncomfortable silence I faced from my class was more so for me than for them. They were, I believe, generally feeling good—but having trouble thinking about my question. They labored to shift from laughing to thinking. My question then led to another moment of silence. They were still feeling good, I did not feel good at all.

The second moment of silence lasted perhaps 30 seconds. This time it weighed very heavily upon me. I had felt very much deflated by their laughter. I still could not think clearly. And yet, as I looked at their faces, I felt connected to them. In asking them what they were thinking, they were taking an interest in what I was thinking. I began to feel more comfortable by gazing at their faces. I slowly regained my ability to think and interact.

I decided that I would simply tell them what I was thinking. I told them that I had the feeling that if I were to argue now that Marx's ideas were innovative contributions to social progress, most of them would dismiss the argument as crazy. I saw some general nods of agreement and some gleeful expressions. I sensed that they had an interest in what I would think. I now felt firmly reestablished to the social link between us.

Conclusion

Clinical literature has explored in great detail relations between emotion and thought. Books and journals published for mental health clinicians, however, are not normal reading for teachers. This is too bad. Therapists may spend two or more years working to help a patient think a single frightening thought. They recognize that humans need help to experience thoughts that threaten their identity pattern. People find themselves in unhappy circumstances because although they recognize that they are suffering, they are unable to develop a mode of thinking that can free them from their suffering. A therapist is hired to help with this thinking. To this end, the mental health discipline has a scholarly literature that describes patterns of helpful and unhelpful emotional engagement with thought. Practitioners learn to be attentive to particular moments of anxiety and curiosity when thought can be effectively appropriated.

It is time for the scholarship on pedagogy to make a similar contribution toward understanding the emotional context important for the assimilation of new information. It is clear to all of us that information contrary to established beliefs does not enter into the thinking machinery of human beings without resistance. A complex set of activities police the boundary that separates undesired corrective information from recognition effects. All teachers, I suspect, work tacitly with the emotional assimilation of information. If we can develop a literature that helps us understand these experiences, we can do our work more effectively. Jennifer Seibel Trainor suggests that we develop a scholarship of "Critical Emotion Studies." I would like to promote this activity and suggest that it work in terms of both theory and narrative analysis of real teaching experiences of the sort that I will present here.

Thought that is powerfully linked to emotion, to a history of emotion, and to a history of a body moved by strong emotional content is not moved by a thought with no emotional links or roots. Thought that effectively assimilates new information has an effect on the emotional body of the thinker. Such thought effectively adapts an emotional and embodied person to new registers of action made possible by thought. In this complex internal emotional readjustment, what is changed is not what thought represents, but how thought is connected to personal motives for action. Effectively assimilated information generates motives for action; new information is linked to the body and its feelings, to its emotional history of feelings, and to its feelings about a future world.

Thought can change quickly, but the emotional body does not adapt quickly to new information. To work with the emotional ground of thought requires work on the body of emotion over time. This work often involves an ongoing spontaneous response to evolving emotional contexts and an ongoing reflective engagement with the emotions that initially shape and create bias in response. Work on the emotional body means particular attention to experiences of shame and pride. The presence of these feelings may not be available for recognition in a single moment of reflection.

If emotion and reason are in fact inseparable, as recent research demonstrates, we must develop a research program to understand the particular nature of these links. We must develop a theory, a vocabulary, a method of study, and a body of literature that can give teachers particular accounts of how these factors work.

Chapter Three
Symptomatic Fixation, Emotion, and Social Alliance

Made popular by Freud, the term "symptom" has become widely used to describe oddly motivated and inflexibly repetitive habits of thought. One does not need to know anything about therapy or mental health to see how some individuals, "fixated" upon deeply held beliefs, determinedly deny all rational evidence contradicting such belief. A March 2011 article on the paranoia of American politics in the *New Internationalist Magazine* discusses three prominent but dubious beliefs still in currency: that the World Trade Center bombings were orchestrated by the American government itself; that health vaccines are the result of a conspiracy within the pharmaceutical industry; and that Obama was born in Kenya and not Hawaii. One of the more interesting (though less popular) claims has been proposed by David Icke, a former UK soccer player, TV personality, and one time Green Party spokesperson. He suggests that George Bush, along with Queen Elizabeth, Prince Charles, Tony Blair, Kris Kristofferson, and American country singer Boxcar Willie are all members of an élite illuminati—shape-shifting, multidimensional, blood-drinking alien reptiles—who have been controlling humanity for centuries. David Icke's website, http://www.davidicke.com/, struggles somewhat defiantly to offer evidence in support.

Human beings have long recognized that other human beings can have "oddly fixed ideas." They hold on to particular cherished ideas against all opposition. For the most part Americans are unsure about how to respond to such claims. On the one hand, America is a free country and everyone has a right to his or her own opinion. And thus we have a certain tendency to be tolerant. On the other hand, America is a democracy and the life of the country depends upon informed public debate. We can find ourselves in conditions where we very passionately attempt to persuade another person of the falsity of their belief and we discover that the debate seems oddly unresponsive to evidence.

Genuine public debate requires that evidence be able, in principle, to move people in their rational commitment to ideas and positions. Evidence addresses humans in their core capacity to be free—to choose what is best. The very recognition of a category of thought that might be termed "evidence" signals an emotional investment in a highly optimistic social ideal. Evidence is an anchor for concepts such as democracy, reasoned public debate, and free will.

Educators explore and distribute facts; educators teach principles of logic and reason. Educators assume that evidence, in and of itself, will be persuasive. But there are people who deny both facts and reason and cling tenaciously to unsupported belief. It is useful to recognize particular situations where thought develops and tenaciously insists impervious to the influence of evidence.

True fixations of belief that deny evidence are not thought, but failures of thought. They are symptomatic fixations and should be understood as such. They are mental symptoms, patterns of mindless repetition unresponsive to the dialectical complexities of evidence and reason. Just as a psychotic is unable to respond to the demands of evidence and logical thought, so also are many beliefs similarly fixated. We encounter these beliefs in the classroom, in the public sphere, and in interpersonal relations. They are instances of a desire not to know that cannot be addressed in terms of logical reasoning.

Teachers, by and large, have no criteria for distinguishing between what I term the "symptomatic fixations" of frozen ideas and the flexible rationality of real thought. In this chapter I will explore a continuum of behaviors that represent two poles of an emotional dialectic that attends to new and uncomfortable information. One pole, which I will term "symptomatic fixation," is seen in minds that, on particular issues, are unable to respond without the simple repetition of established belief. I am calling these non-dialectical responses "symptomatic" following Freud's use of the term. Some aspect of belief operates as a kernel of ideation, immune from the influence of external reality. This tightly organized network of discourse is immune to any oppositional dialectic. No amount of evidence, reality testing, social interaction, or evidence evaluation can have an impact on such ideation.

A second form of resistance to uncomfortable information is emotionally slow to take in evidence, but it does respond to an emotional dialectic. I term this second condition "emotional resistance," which I take to be a description already in circulation, though often used as a recognition of the limits of thought rather than a term that proposes a strategy for working with the anxiety and fear of emotional change. In cases of emotional resistance, thought is possible, but not in terms of logical processes. It is possible in terms of emotional recontextualization and integration particularly facilitated by new social connections.

I will illustrate these conditions with reference to specific examples: psychotic behavior, neurotic behavior, and fixated political behavior. I will suggest that although symptomatic fixation is not psychotic by definition, it has a similar quality of mindless repetition and anxious defense. A better understanding of symptomatic fixation will allow teachers to recognize this quality more quickly and respond to it more effectively.

The second condition, a state of "emotional resistance," represents situations where people resist new ideas, but also show a capacity for engagement with this information. All of us are slow to take in information when this information challenges our values. The mind is not a computer that can instantly compute all information encountered. Much information has to be "processed" over time and in changing emotional contexts in order for the implications of the information to be integrated.

I have argued at length elsewhere (Alcorn 2001) that one common example of resistance to new information is seen in situations of significant loss. Almost no one accepts immediately the news of the loss of a close relation, parent, lover, partner, spouse. Information about the loss, for example, of a beloved parent, is immediately experienced with an insistence upon the remembered presence of that parent. We hold on to the memory of the parent, often in outright opposition to the evidential truth of death. Freud (1917) described mourning as work on memory. He described two features of this process. First, new information cannot be integrated with old information until work is done on the body of memory. Second, this "work" done on memory is painful and proceeds slowly over time as it requires giving up attachments to a much-loved figure. After loss, old memories have to be reworked and reorganized, and this work takes time and psychic energy.

To illustrate the emotional complexity of information assimilation I discuss particular situations of mental stress—trauma and grief— where new information is never easily processed. Judith Herman defines trauma as that which cannot be mourned (1982). Trauma presents a case where information assimilation becomes part of an ongoing emotional struggle. Stories of trauma describe how information, not known by the conscious mind, is stored in dissociated areas of memory and exert an impact on daily life. In its most extreme forms, trauma can be like a psychotic experience. Dead friends are hallucinated. Past dangers are defended in inappropriate new contexts. The hypervigilance of trauma triggers defensive responses in self-destructive patterns. I will refer to trauma in describing some of the problems associated with unintegrated memory. At one extreme, trauma can be the first step of a mourning process that works to integrate new information. At the other extreme, trauma can be an encysted network of memory (a symptom) with psychotic indifference to new information.

My goal is to describe recognizable features of mind that are resistant or impervious to evidence. I argue that minds with symptomatic fixation are minds unable to integrate memory and thus unable to make use of new information. Traumatized minds often exhibit this character, and we can observe that this dynamic is oddly similar to the character of psychosis. Ramachandran, for example, describes patients who have lost the use of a limb but hallucinate its presence. Some of these patients demonstrate a psychotic-like inability to see what is in front of them and a psychotic-like inability to take in new information.

Today most people do recognize psychosis as an illness characterized by symptomatic fixation: the illness expresses ideas that cannot be changed through evidence or reason. Such recognition, however, is fairly recent. Just as the fixated beliefs of psychosis can be misunderstood, so also many everyday classroom examples of symptomatic fixation are misunderstood. Idealistic teachers seek to reason with minds that have no capacity to reason, just as Milton Rokeach, in the narrative that follows, insisted upon evidence and reason to persuade three psychotics that they were not Jesus Christ.

Varieties of Symptomatic Fixation

In 1959, Rokeach, a social psychologist in Ward D-23 of the Ypsilanti State Hospital, Michigan, was inspired by French philosopher Voltaire to cure psychosis through reason. As an Enlightenment thinker, Voltaire had a deep faith in the power of reason and felt his belief in reason challenged by the condition of madness. He sought to understand what it might mean. In his *Philosophical Dictionary*, he considers madness simply a condition of the soul and he asks: "If this simple and eternal substance enjoys the same properties as the souls which are lodged in the sagest brains, it ought to reason like them. Why does it not?" (Voltaire [1764b] 1901).

Milton Rokeach was impressed with Voltaire's discussion of a case where the madness of one Simon Morin, was allegedly for a time, cured by simple logic. When Morin encountered, in a madhouse, a madman with a belief similar to his own, he was (so the story goes) brought to his sense by simple logic. He recognized that since only one person could be God, and since another man clearly claimed to be God, then he, Morin, could not be God. Voltaire narrates the story thus:

> Imagining that he had seen visions, he carried his folly so far, as to believe that he was sent from God, and that he was incorporated with Jesus Christ.
>
> The Parliament very wisely condemned him to be confined in a mad-house. What was very remarkable, there happened to be confined in the same mad-house another fool, who called himself God the Father. Simon Morin was so struck with the folly of his companion, that he acknowledged his own, and appeared for a time to have recovered his senses. (Voltaire [1764a] 1872)

Intrigued by Voltaire's story, Rokeach attempted to use argumentation and reason to cure three psychotics who believed that they were God or Christ. Three severely disturbed men were brought together daily for group discussion. Clyde Benson, aged 70, a former carpenter, farm laborer, and alcoholic, had been hospitalized for 17 years. Joseph Cassel, 58, former clerk and failed writer, had been hospitalized for ten years. Leon Gabor, 38, a college dropout who had served effectively in the army during World War II, had been hospitalized for five years.

After two years of almost daily work Rokeach ended his experiment by suggesting that perhaps he was as delusional as his patients in thinking that he could "play God" by using reason (Rokeach 1964, xiii). I want to emphasize here a theme that emerges in each chapter of this book. Many of us fail to recognize the limits of reason. There is a consistent and abiding delusion that resistant people can be brought to change their ideas by patient or impatient insistence upon reason and evidence.

Many beliefs held by apparently "normal" people have a psychotic-like resistance to logic, reason, and social interaction. If Ramachandran's generalizations about denial are correct, we should consider that many common instances of determined denial are similar to the failures of perception and reason in psychotics. Rokeach introduces his book on the three psychotics with a quote from Bertrand Russell: "Everyman would like to be God, if it were possible; some few find it difficult to admit this impossibility" (1938, 3). Like Ramachandran Rokeach spent much time working with what appeared to be extreme cases of mental imbalance, only to conclude that extreme cases are helpful representations of everyday, though less dramatic, thought. Most people, of course, do not publicly claim to be God. But we have reliable evidence (Nyhan and Reifler 2010) that many people have a grandiose ability to deny facts and insist on the truth of their beliefs. If the condition of being God is not adjusting to reality but changing reality, then all of us aspire to this condition. In this sense, the desire not to know is a small concession to everyday grandiose temptations.

We see evidence of fixated beliefs every day; we need only look more closely to understand the "logic" of these attachments. In a novel written just before the turn of the twentieth century, Joseph Conrad's fictional narrator, Marlow, offers an apt description of a clearly fixated and thus "symptomatic" belief:

> I knew once a Scotch sailmaker who was certain, dead sure, there were people in Mars. If you asked him for some idea how they looked and behaved he would get shy and mutter something about "walking on all-fours." If you as much as smiled he would—though a man of sixty—offer to fight you. ([1899] 1988, 29)

There are two bits of evidence here to suggest that this sailmaker's belief is more than a reasonable deduction derived from a preponderance of evidence. First, the sailmaker is remarkably, even aggressively certain of a fact he is unable to support by means of concrete evidence. Second, he is extremely anxious and defensive in regard to this claim he seems unable to support. "Though a man of sixty," he is quick to fight to support a certainty that apparently lacks other means for support. He is particularly sensitive to personal insult, and he recognizes, when questioned, that his claims need support in order to be held as certain. But he is unable to make any defense of his position other than that of pure bodily aggression. These two qualities—lack of rational support and hostile bodily defensiveness—are characteristic of symptomatic thinking

Freud's understanding of the symptom is helpful for understanding broader relations among symptoms and discourse circulation. In "Inhibitions, Symptoms and Anxiety," Freud describes symptoms as produced by defensive processes that generate repression. As the purpose of the symptom is to defend the self from anxiety, any attempt to bring "truth to light" increases anxiety and strengthens the defense against truth. More reason does not liberate a symptom from falsehood; it increases the irrational fixity of the symptom. Later in the chapter I will review research that demonstrates how corrective information intensifies commitments to false political beliefs.

The symptom has its ground, not in language, reality, and rational meaning, but in anxiety. The symptom is a response to anxiety. It is an irrational response because it does nothing to protect the bodily self from danger. But while it does not protect a biological body from danger, it does protect a psychological "body" from the anxiety that would attend the awareness of an unpleasant fact.

One of the psychotics treated by Rokeach, Joseph Cassel, wrote to one of his daughters: "I am prince and God and keeper of the courts. This is the truth. I have civilized the whole world. I am aeons and aeons of years old. I'm the richest man in the world and England" (Rokeach 1964, 45). When his oldest daughter learned of his claims she reported: "He always wanted to be important, better than other people" (ibid.). When Leon Gabor, another psychotic, read an article in *Newsweek* about Rokeach's plan to confront the men with the "ultimate contradiction," he "became angry and brought the session to an end by saying he had to go to the toilet" (Rokeach 1964, 166). Cassel's daughter believed her father held grandiose beliefs to feel good about himself. Gabor responds to the threat to his ideational system by a bodily urge to evacuate internal objects, to void urine or feces. Gabor's body expresses a contempt for the *Newsweek* article that he himself does not verbalize.

This relation between the symptom and anxiety becomes particularly important for the teacher because it means that any attempt to undo a symptom can have a similar effect of releasing anxiety. When teachers attempt to "prove" the falsehood of a belief that is purely symptomatic, the proof will function as nothing more than a release of often-unbearable anxiety. The old sailmaker threatens to fight; Leon is angry and needs to go to the toilet; a student may remain silent but will experience feelings of hostility and deny whatever logical or evidentiary material the teacher tries to introduce.

In teaching, we encounter at least two different mental acts that support knowledge. We encounter rational truth claims that are open to dialogical elaboration and we also encounter symptomatic fixations that resist dialogical elaboration. A symptomatic fixation has the same verbal form as a truth claim, but it is not the same. Truth claims respond effortlessly to the pressure of demonstration and logical argument. Symptomatic fixations are intertwined with the body's biological expressions of emotions, particulary emotion of anger, shame, and anxiety.

Consider the example of a person who chooses, through a phobia, to avoid public swimming pools because he is afraid he may be eaten by sharks. Imagine telling this person that there is really nothing to fear in the pool. It may be obviously true that there are no sharks or crocodiles hiding in public swimming pools. Nonetheless, phobic swimmers may imagine these animals to be present. And if you insist that the pool is perfectly safe, your insistence only increases their anxiety. They will likely have the experience that you are making them unsafe.

A symptomatic belief is not banished easily by what we consider "proof." A person with a symptom can believe that there are sharks in a public pool, and feel compelled to act on their beliefs, even though they also "know," in some sense, that there are no sharks in the pool. Clinical experience repeatedly demonstrates that knowledge does not easily change the symptoms expressed by people in therapy. What is important to understand is that the verbal insistence, "There are no sharks in the pool," meant to reassure the person of their safety, in fact increases their anxiety. The truth assertion makes them feel less safe, less able in fact to think.

The implication of this is important for teachers. It suggests that working on rational evidence can actually impair the resistant student's ability to reason.

I once had a student who wrote about her fear that she would be eaten by sharks if she stepped on the wooden floor of her bedroom. She had gone to see the movie *Jaws*, and after she came home she developed an unbearable fear of her bedroom floor. She knew of course that there were no sharks hidden in the wood of her floor. But even though she "knew" this to be true, she still feared sharks might eat her if she stepped on the floor of her room. Interestingly, her own report of her experience indicated that she easily held two incompatible beliefs in her mind simultaneously. She could think the reasonable thought that sharks do not live in wooden floors. This reasonable thought could diminish her anxiety about sharks. Perhaps sharks did not live in wooden floors, but nonetheless she feared that if she walked on a wooden floor a shark might eat her.

My student told this story in my classroom, and when she tried to explain what happened, some students laughed. She herself was very tense and serious. She described how she had moved her bed as close to the door of her room as possible and had spread the floor with her stuffed animals. But she still could not move from the bed to the door without walking over some wood in the floor. And this move terrified her. After a day of terror, her parents took her to a therapist. Over time her fear of sharks in the floor disappeared.

This story indicates some of the relations existing between knowledge and irrational fears or desires we see in symptoms. Truth claims, no matter how true, no matter how well supported by established facts, do not change symptomatic behavior and belief. Teachers see this kind of resistance to evidence on an almost daily basis, but they commonly interpret this resistance as a kind of moral flaw that can be overcome by more determined logical reasoning. In failing to think about these problems, we impede the life of reason. We are unreasonable in our commitment to reason.

In chapter two I suggested that some verbal statements such as "President Obama was born in Africa," may not be thought, but expressions of attachment. The brain is operating, as in the patients with anosognosia, to affirm an unthreatened self. Verbal statements often assert symptomatic fantasies of security. Thinking responds to dialectical complication; symptomatic fixation does not. Many "opinions" are not strictly speaking "thoughts," and we should not act as if thoughtful engagements with such statements can magically liberate thought from falsehood. Just as Rokeach learned that he could not cure psychosis through reason and evidence, we need to learn when we cannot cure symptomatic fixations by reason and evidence.

Freud used the term "symptom" to explain deficiencies in mental life resulting from "trauma." I propose that our current understanding of trauma—and its relation to the symptom—can help explain the deficiencies in evidence integration observed in the true believers of Stanley Fish. Fish argues that belief is justified by what he terms "a lattice or web whose component parts are mutually constitutive" (1999, 280). Olson and Worsham argue that Fish's structure of belief can "more accurately be termed an ideoaffective structure" (2001,155).

In using the term "ideoaffective structure," Olson and Worsham suggest that heartfelt beliefs do not happen by sheer accident. They follow an emotional logic. In "Going Postal: Pedagogic Violence and the Schooling of Emotion," Lynn Worsham argues that we are all educated by violence in institutions such as the school, the workplace, and the family. Violence, because of our need to provide a defence against it, is commonly the organizing force behind mental organization. Violence, both personal and social, is an impetus to the creation of beliefs that operate, as Fish claims, like "a lattice or web whose component parts are mutually constitutive" (1999, 280). Worsham's concept of an "ideoaffective structure" offers, on the one hand, a principle for understanding symptoms, with their tenacious and repetitive invulnerability to dialectic, and, on the other hand, a principle for understanding the general logic of mental organization itself—an interaction between thought and emotion.

Worsham's attention to educative violence calls attention to common developmental experiences that disorganize the mind at the same time as they organize it. It may well be that the mind's organizational response to violence sets in place a kind of traumatic rigidity of belief. On the one hand, a traumatic experience creates a defensive web of mutually interconnected feelings, beliefs, and verbal claims. On the other hand, a traumatic experience isolates this web from the developmental opportunities of new information.

Traumatic memory does not function as everyday memory. Memories from the past are hypervigilant in their attention to present experience. Information from present reality is irrelevant and not assimilated. It is as if there are isolated knots of verbal insistence or belief that are supremely invulnerable to any kind of rational intervention. Freud talked about trauma as mental conflict, as knotted and incompatible feelings, memories, and thoughts. In more contemporary terms we can say that trauma dissociates memory. Contemporary neuroscience describes trauma as a trigger for irrationally persistent actions and beliefs. Louis Cozolino writes:

> Healthy functioning requires proper development and functioning of neural networks organizing conscious awareness, behavior, emotion, and sensation... Unresolved trauma results in information processing deficits that disrupt integrated neural processing... Children victimized by psychological, physical and sexual abuse have a greater probability of demonstrating electro-physiological abnormalities in executive regions of the brain vital to neural network integration. (2002, 21)

People who suffer from trauma suffer from deficiencies in memory organization and integration much like Ramachandran's patients with anosognosia.

In the examples of Ramachandran's patients, of my student who feared her bedroom floor, and of Conrad's Scotch sailmaker, the features of the symptom are similar. There is a stubborn attachment to some belief or behavior that seems irrational and maladaptive. Attempts to talk to the person to shift thinking are unsuccessful. Talking does produce a dialogue; both partners to the discussion can produce words. But the person on the symptomatic side of the dialogue cannot modify their position on the basis of the alleged "force" of empirical evidence, reason, logic, or the clearly perceivable evidence of present reality.

In severe cases of trauma one can see, through brain scans, reduced neurological links between the right and left sides of the brain. Trauma presents problems to information assimilation because it reduces links between areas of the brain that process information. But not all trauma can be seen in brain scans. If we seek to make a clear distinction between trauma and the various shocks of grief and loss we will find that the line between the two situations is obscure.

Most teachers, I suspect, imagine that symptoms are visible in people seeking clinical help and thinking is visible in classroom discussion. It is useful to reverse this picture. Clinical settings are places where much thinking takes place and classrooms are spaces where symptomatic thinking characteristically takes place. Clinicians generally have good intuitions regarding the relation between thought and emotion. They make use of emotion to promote thought. We may imagine a sharp boundary between "crazy" thinking, which puts people into asylums, and sane thinking, which goes on in everyday life. This imagined boundary may protect us from anxiety, but no such boundary exists.

Teachers, by and large, do not understand relations between thought and emotion. They can "instinctively" demand "thought" at times when emotional context makes it impossible. The demand for thought, however well intentioned, can be experienced as a "violence" that makes thought impossible rather than possible. If a symptomatic fixation is a traumatic attachment that cannot be mourned, then a demand to abandon the attachment can only be experienced as traumatic.

Everyday Symptomatic Fixation

Let us consider symptom fixation as any irrational belief a person repeats, defends by dismissal, or defends with hostility. Symptomatic thinking opposes flexible thinking. Flexible thinking desires reason, evidence, and patient exploration of logical relations. Symptomatic thinking does not. Many modes of thinking that we do not normally consider as symptoms have clear symptomatic features.

I once had a classroom interaction with a student who claimed that people should believe authority figures without question. When I heard this assertion I was a surprised, but I thought I could simply respond to the claim with a few simple, rational questions. I tried to explore the logical range of the generalization she had made. Would she agree that in all cases people should obey authority figures without question, or only in some cases? To my astonishment, and to the astonishment of everyone else in class, she argued that in all cases people should obey authority figures without question. As soon as she got these words out of her mouth, ten hands went up in the classroom. Many other students wanted to question the wisdom of this.

The class had been very relaxed. The students were mostly women. They seldom engaged in direct argument. They were usually generous with each other's thinking. This comment, however, generated pointed interest and response. I did not know then what I know now about working with symptomatic thought. I focused hard and somewhat relentlessly on logical reason to see if I could change the student's thinking or, as I represented it internally, "push this student to think."

I started to ask the usual questions that might come to mind (and there were many). "Was it good that the average German citizen of 1939 did not question the actions of the ruler of Germany?" To whatever question I posed, she simply repeated her assertion. "People should obey authority figures without question." I had the sense that she herself at this point was feeling both stuck and embarrassed, but she "chose" (and I now put this word within quotation marks to signal my possible misreading) to repeat her claims without modifications. I asked her to define the properties that gave "authority" to particular people and institutions. She responded by repeating her earlier claim.

I tried to find other ways to work with her logic. I suggested that perhaps what she was really thinking was something about obedience rather than belief. Perhaps she meant that people should prudently "obey" authority figures, even if they had some doubts. It was much easier to argue that people had an obligation to obey authority than to believe it. To suggest that people should never even "question" authority seemed extreme. My suggestion did not move her. "People should not question authority figures," she argued.

In my eagerness to find the right mode of reasoning, I hit upon what is experienced as a triumphal contradiction. "If I, as a teacher and authority figure, ask her to question authority, should she do as I say?" "Authority figures are your parents," she finally said, neatly removing me from the category of authority figures. This opened up a new set of terms, and I, and other students, sought to make sense of this new formulation. But after a few minutes of interaction, we all gave up. We simply went on with the day's material. It was as if we were all thinking, "Okay this is crazy, but everyone is entitled to his or her own opinion. So let's just go on." I suspect that many of us respond in this manner.

I now believe that we can better understand encounters such as this. There are better responses than the generous "everyone is entitled to his or her own opinion." If a student claims, "I am against paying taxes to feed the poor," or "People should believe authority figures," we might wonder if this position may be something like a symptomatic fixation. If symptoms function as strategic and dumbly repetitive modes of defense against anxiety, we can easily imagine that a vast range of discourse has the structure of a symptom. It is useful to be able to recognize such action as not "thought" but symptomatic fixation. If cases of symptomatic fixation could be identified and understood, we would be in a better position, as a culture, to make progress in solving problems through reason.

When we encounter situations where students are unable to respond to the pressures of evidence and reason, we profit from understanding the particular emotional connections in the resistance we face. Some emotional resistances are moved by appropriate emotional responses. Other resistances are unmoved. We can manage our resources if we understand what we face. Some verbal claims with anxious and repetitive qualities are not "one way to think" but a failure to think. We can develop responses that do not demand logical thought, but explore networks of emotional attachment. It is useful for all of us to know the emotional attachments we have.

We can postulate that much political "knowledge" on both the left and the right has the structure of symptomatic fixation. Many political truth claims are assertions of symptomatic fixation. Recent research in political science suggests that symptomatic fixations are widespread.

In 2007 John Sides and Jack Critin ran tests to see how supplying facts might change the beliefs of people who held incorrect ideas about immigration. These researchers found that very often when people were given correct information regarding the proportion of immigrants in the United States, their political beliefs did not change to adjust to the new information.

In a similar but somewhat different study, James Kuklinski et al. (2000) of the University of Illinois at Urbana-Champaign questioned one thousand Illinois residents about welfare. Kuklinski and his colleagues asked participants in the study questions about the system. The group asked about the percentage of the federal budget spent on welfare, the number of people enrolled in the program, the percentage of enrollees who are black, and the average payout. More than half of the participants in the study giving answers insisted their answers were correct. Kuklinski found, however, that only 3 percent of the people tested on the information got more than half of the questions right. What was most dramatic was the discovery that the people who were the *most* confident about what they knew, in fact knew the least.

In 2010 political scientists Brendan Nyhan and Jason Reifler tested how misinformed citizens respond to factual corrections. The motive for their experiment is clear: "It is especially important to determine whether misperceptions, which distort public opinion and political debate, can be corrected" (Nyhan and Reifler 2010, 304). They conducted four different experiments in which they gave participants mock newspaper articles containing a misleading claim and then later gave participants a correction of that claim. They report on their results as follows:

> In each of the four experiments, which were conducted in fall 2005 and spring 2006, ideological subgroups failed to update their beliefs when presented with corrective information that runs counter to their predispositions. Indeed, in several cases, we find that corrections actually strengthened misperceptions among the most strongly committed subjects. (Nyhan and Reifler 2010, 304)

Nyhan and Reifler term this pattern of sheer resistance to the evidence a "backfire effect" (2010, 303). An encounter with evidence against their belief makes these people believe ever more strongly. If democracies allow all people with "backfire" responses to evidence the status of rational actors, they fail. I do not propose that we seek to deprive some people of the right to vote, but that we observe the behavior we see in "thinking" and give useful descriptions to behavior that shows a failure of thought. I do not want to intimidate people with labels; I do want to make visible patterns that would otherwise remain invisible.

A problem-solving mind would be interested in information, of whatever implication. This mind would respond to evidence with a suitable depth of reflection and attentive processing of contradictory evidence. This mind would acknowledge a multitude of possible facts and inquire into their reliability and applicability. It would desire to know more circumstantial facts about the purported facts. This mind would also seek to evaluate evidence rather than insistently dismiss it.

In theory, the difference between rational thinking and symptomatic fixation can be tested by the introduction of evidence. In the case of a student symptomatically asserting that the poor are responsible for their own condition, a teacher could test the student's response to evidence. If no amount of evidence that the poor do not easily find work changes the degree of insistence in the student's mind, we should be suspicious. What is at stake in this belief is not a judgment about facts, but anxiety and irrational fears that resolve themselves in a compromise formation that analysts call symptoms. If a student is able to offer counterevidence or qualify generalizations, we are working with a thoughtful student.

The symptom is an expression of knotted emotions that supports an assertion termed "knowledge" in a tenaciously non-dialectical manner. If a student can counter evidence against the claim with evidence for the claim or with a critique of the evidentiary claims, the student is in fact thinking. But if the presentation of evidence leads to mere repetition without elaboration, the statement does not demonstrate thinking but symptomatic fixation. The student in this case "knows" that everyone in America can be successful, but this verbal claim expresses symptomatic fixation.

We are a long way from being able to test congressmen and presidential candidates for traumatic fixations that preclude their ability to take in new information. We do not yet have evidence to generalize that everyday denial is the result of biological impediments. But we do have evidence to suggest that the brain works according to biological principles very different from the instant logical calculations of a computer. For humans, all thought is not possible at all times. We need to be more flexible in recognizing and understanding apparently "unbelievable" examples of "stupidity."

We improve our ability to recognize symptomatic thinking in the classroom. The concept of symptomatic fixation can help us recognize and manage the frustrations that we often feel as teachers, confronted with what seems to be an unbelievable moment of resistance. I do want to offer a cautionary warning about this. It is very easy for teachers, frustrated with students who disagree, to intimidate them with greater factual knowledge and more complex reasoning. It is tempting as well, for teachers to label some students as "symptomatically fixated." Such a label, however, will do little to actually improve a student's capacity to reason. The point is not to use the label, but to understand when, where, and how it is possible to work with fixation. In addition, thinking about symptomatic fixation is itself a form of thinking that needs to be both flexible and dialogic. Teachers should invite students to observe the degree of flexibility in their own thinking as well. They too will find themselves locked, at times, in such practices.

Symptomatic Fixation and Emotional Relation

Rokeach begins his experiment with psychotics by seeking to address the sheer force of reason. He ended his experiment declaring a greater appreciation for the emotional dialectics of thought and social interaction. Students come to class with particular histories. But classrooms often become places where emotional themes develop and become subjects for contemplation. Bion argues that human thought begins as the representation of human relationship. It is grounded in the binaries of love and hate and moves toward greater sophistication as the intensity of these affects respond more realistically to the features of the world. In Rokeach's work with psychotics, it is clear that emotional responses to human relationships change how symptomatic fixations are expressed.

Rokeach hoped that if his three psychotic patients confronted each other and talk about their beliefs and their thinking about themselves, they might eventually grasp the logical problems of maintaining their beliefs. Rokeach found that logical argument did nothing to change these men's beliefs. He did find, though, that the emotional interactions of the meetings contributed to change.

Rokeach planned for these men to confront the "ultimate contradiction conceivable for human beings: more than one person claiming the same identity." He believed that if he gave his patients enough evidence and patient reasoning they might come to see the error of their ways or experience some improvement in their condition. He met with his patients daily over two years, drawing attention to their shared assertions to be Christ, and presenting as much evidence as he could that such a belief was false. Aristotle, ever the great rhetorician, argued that truth is always easier to prove than falsehood because there is always more evidence for the truth than there is for falsehood (Aristotle 2004, 6). Rokeach certainly found plenty of proof that these men were not Christ. At one point, one of the men turns his back on a massive table and commands that it be lifted. Rokeach, who observes this, says that he does not see the table being lifted. He is told, "Sir that is because you do not see cosmic reality" (Rokeach 1964, 75).

These men, subjected to the appeals of reason, experienced a degree of emotional anxiety and conflict in the first three weeks of the experiment. Rokeach could observe sharp disagreements and emotional discomfort. They were able to see and experience logical contradictions in their respective claims. They were quarrelsome, but in a generally restrained manner. Surprisingly their conflicts became more restrained as time went on. Rokeach observes: "At least on the surface the intent seemed to be to persuade each other and to impress everyone, including us, with the fact that they were reasonable men who could talk things over" (Rokeach 1964, 53). These psychotics, brought together as a group with sharply conflicting beliefs, were able to manage their contradictions through a pattern of daily interaction.

Three weeks into the experiment there was an outbreak of violence, but not over claims about which of the men is in fact Jesus Christ. The disagreement, oddly, was over what would appear to be a logically subordinate issue: race. Leon makes a statement that "Adam was a colored man." Clyde disagrees. "Adam was white, I made the passing of that at one year old" (Rokeach 1964, 59). It is noteworthy that the literal issue of the disagreement, race, seems negligible in relation to the larger logical claims about who is God. It is as if these psychotics are more prone to a violence triggered by cultural symptoms of racial bias than by personal symptoms of psychotic behavior.

Over time, conflict among the men diminishes and we see them engage in processes of reasoning to minimize the logical contradictions that the experience presents them with. Clyde explains the contradictions between his claim of being God and the claims of others by asserting that the other two men, Joseph and Leon, are "really not alive." "The machines in them are talking" (Rokeach 1964, 51). Joseph asserts, rather reasonably, that the other two men, Leon and Clyde, are "insane." He has evidence for this argument; they are in an mental asylum. Leon gave numerous and different accounts of the claims made by the other men, but he, unlike the other two, seemed to feel that there was some truth in their claims.

He grants them some nominal divinity. He claims that the others are "hollowed out instrumental gods with a small 'g.'" We can see a use of language here that seems to perform a useful logical function. Leon insists upon the supremacy of his own God-like power, but he also offers to grant some God-like quality to the others as "instrumental gods."

After two years it becomes clear to Rokeach that his plan to stage an "ultimate confrontation" will never take place. What begins as an experiment with logical thought becomes instead an interesting experiment with psychotic social interaction.

Rokeach comes to think that gathering these lonely men together to talk offers them possibilities for social connection that they value very much. After some time, he decides to give the men the freedom to control their meetings. He discovers that the men seem to enjoy being with each other. They adapt to the conflicts in their own differing identity claims by not talking about them. Rather than working through the logical contradictions, they ignore them. Over the course of the experiment, the two older men showed no change. The younger man, Leon, showed no change in his core beliefs, but he does begin to speak about himself differently. He granted a degree of verbal recognition of divinity to the others. He also changed his name from God and Christ to Rex and Dung. He asks to be called by these names by others. He seems to feel a desire to make adjustments in his identity and his verbal claims change.

For psychotics, as well as for others, an enormous amount of emotion—desire, anxiety, fear, and hope—are invested in attachments to identity. Psychotic attachments seem almost invulnerable to the force of logical thought. In Rokeach's account of work at the Ypsilanti State Hospital, the younger man, Leon, showed some modestly dramatic changes after many months of interacting with the other psychotics. His most dramatic changes, though, were the results of emotional responses to people in his environment to whom he was most attached, his wife, and a female attendant. After getting a letter from his wife, Leon tries to restrain his sadness, but finally cries what Rokeach describes as "two tears." This emotional expression has consequences. Leon cries, and then changes an established pattern. He spends money for the first time on himself and on others. Rokeach observes: "All these changes were potentially of great therapeutic value... He had allowed himself to feel, to express, for once, a human emotion" (1964, 223).

In therapy rational thought is facilitated by what is termed the "therapeutic alliance." Many studies indicate that the success of a therapy correlates strongly with the emotional bond that is developed between the patient and the therapist. According to Daniel Martin, John Garske, and Katherine Davis:

> In the past two decades, psychotherapy researchers and practitioners have postulated that the therapeutic alliance—defined broadly as the collaborative and affective bond between therapist and patient—is an essential element of the therapeutic process. Although the alliance concept originated in early psychoanalytic theories... it has become increasingly common in recent conceptualizations of the therapeutic process generally. The primary reason the alliance has grown in significance is the consistent finding that the quality of the alliance is related to subsequent therapeutic outcome. (2000, 438)

Bonds between teachers and students often develop similarly to bonds between therapists and patients. The concept of the therapeutic alliance helps describe how progress in rational thought is facilitated by forming new social bonds. Students form alliances with teachers and they form alliances with other students. Outside therapy, many different alliances among people allow cognitive growth and improved mental flexibility.

One characteristic of the liberal arts experience that students particularly value is the effectiveness of a personal relationship between the teacher and the student. Peter Filene, professor of History at University of North Carolina and winner of six teaching awards, reminds us that "when you teach, you are engaging in a relationship with your students" (2005, 2). He continues:

> Teaching is a two way process that educators call "dialogic." An instructor talks, but what do his or her students hear and understand? Teaching is only as successful as the learning it produces. Indeed, the teaching learning relationship is not simply dialogic, between professor and students, but polylogic, among students too. They may learn from each other, or intimidate each other, but positively or negatively, tacitly or explicitly, they play their role in the pedagogical relationship. (Filene 2005, 3)

New social bonds, working to produce new emotional contexts and experiences, can have the potential to open up forms of thought that have been held in place by authoritarian allegiances that restrict the free play of thought.

If new social bonds open up new possibilities for thought, it is also true that existing social bonds can work to close down possibilities for thought.

In Norman Mailer's Pulitzer Prize-winning novel, *The Naked and the Dead*, the narrator frequently reports on the inner state of mind of characters faced with difficult decisions. In one scene the narrator takes us into the inner thoughts of soldiers who have been sent on a very risky reconnaissance mission. The men are led by a sadistic hard driving first sergeant named Croft. He has ordered them to climb a treacherous mountain path after their first lieutenant Hearn, who had wanted the platoon to turn back after an ambush, has been killed. One of the soldiers, Red, persuades a low-ranking sergeant, Martinez, to argue with First Sergeant Croft. Red wants Martinez to change Croft's mind. Of all the men in the platoon, Martinez is the soldier most close to Croft. Martinez, however, is torn between his loyalty to Croft (who is a friend and a higher ranking solider) and his loyalty to the other objects, his life, the other men in platoon, and to his loyalty to reason itself. Mailer's narrative takes us into the factors that impinge on Martinez's thinking.

Most readers see, in Mailer's representation of Martinez, a very simple mind at work, a mind whose principal thought reflects fear of a loss of prestige. Mailer has already revealed to the reader that Martinez has changed, in his own mind, the facts of what has happened in the death of Lieutenant Hearn. There are hints of a racist smear in Mailer's representation of an apparently "primitive," unsophisticated Hispanic mind. Croft had demanded that Martinez lie to Hearn about seeing Japanese troops. Martinez lied. But Martinez does not want to recognize the lie. In part, because he does not want to accept blame for the death of Lieutenant Hearn. The lie contributed to the death by not giving Hearn much needed information he needed to prepare for his patrol. Martinez had scouted the route ahead and seen some Japanese, but he told Hearn that no Japanese had been seen.

Mailer shows us that Martinez does not want to know that he had contributed to Hearn's death. What Martinez "remembers" is very different from what had actually happened. In his internal mind he "remembers" that he had told Hearn he had seen the enemy, but Hearn disbelieved him. Mailer portrays Martinez as a person who does not desire to know the truth. He protects his self-worth by lying to himself and to others.

Mailer leads the reader to think, in the scene between Martinez and Croft, that Martinez should, by every sane appraisal of the situation, demand that the patrol be ended. Croft is insisting upon a reckless forward advance into dangerous mountain paths. Martinez clearly fears that he and others will fall from a cliff or that they too will be shot in an ambush. But when the moment comes when Martinez must honestly face Croft, he is unable to determinedly make the demand that could save his own life as well as the lives of everyone in the patrol. Mailer makes it clear that Martinez fears the loss of his self-esteem more than he fears the loss of his life:

> His loyalty, his friendship, his courage, were all involved. And as he looked into Croft's cold blue eyes he felt the same inadequacy and shabbiness, the same inferiority he always knew when he talked to... a White Protestant. (1960, 538)

When Martinez looks into Croft's eyes, he feels acutely that he cannot bear Croft's contempt for talking honestly and truthfully. Because he cannot bear the shame of Croft's contempt, he lies.

One way to talk about this decision-making process we see in Martinez is that the "calculation" of rational thought gets stuck at a variety of points of emotional attachment. Martinez can think rationally about solving his problems when he is helped to think by other soldiers in his platoon. But when he is face-to-face with a particular authority figure and friend, his thinking stops. He feels one set of emotions talking to his fellow soldiers and another set of emotions talking to his senior in command. In both cases, what he thinks is determined by what he feels.

Mailer's account of a mind struggling to formulate a determined and articulate consciousness and speech in terms of its loyalty to people and to concepts such as friendship, courage, army command, and the threat of catastrophic death expresses not a particular weak mind, but the general processes of mentalization. As author, Mailer is perhaps frustrated with people's inability to see the big picture and take honest responsibility for other people in life-and-death situations. But Mailer's representation of Martinez is a useful depiction of all minds. Shame is particularly powerful in its ability to freeze thought, or to trigger quick defensive anger.

Mailer's representation of Martinez describes all minds pulled in different ways by emotional attachments. We are all often in new situations unable to "comfortably" sort through the various feelings we have on issues. It is as if the weight of each link to a friend holds a pull on the momentum of thought's calculation.

In Mailer's novel, inner thought seems to work, not according to a process of logic, but according to a logic of social attachment and its corresponding feeling. Martinez cannot think about contradicting Cross because he feels a primary attachment to him.

Martinez worries that the patrol is useless and may result in his death. And yet he fears that if he complains, he will lose his friendship with the top sergeant. He has to "feel" his way through what matters most to him. His thinking directly reflects his feeling and it is as if he can only think those ideas that reflect his strongest emotional links. There are many possible thoughts available to him, but he can only think those that do not contradict his strongest allegiance.

Thinking for Martinez, like everyone, is not a rational calculation similar to a computer doing a mathematical calculation. Thinking, instead, requires a sorting through of memory and various emotional claims and alliances. In a context of face-to-face discussion with his fellow soldiers, Martinez feels the emotional pressure of their thought on his thought. In another face-to-face discussion with Croft, Martinez feels the pressure of Croft's point of view. Any synthesis of these conflicting perspectives would have to be done over time as different social relations, and their corresponding emotional contexts, allow the emergence of different thoughts and allow an awareness of the emotional conflicts they reveal. Human thinking slows down, stops, or deflects at the point of emotional attachment; it can swerve oddly at points of emotional conflict.

Emotional Attachment and Mental Representation

About midway in my teaching career I came to feel that classroom discussions seemed to go much better if I let students stake out a variety of positions on an issue and I simply facilitated a thoughtful interaction among students. I had a feeling that students were more able to be thoughtful if they responded not just to my appeals to thought, but to appeals from other students. As I paid more attention to this process I began to feel that this worked well only when students established comfortable relations with each other. This led me to pay more attention to how students listened to each other. I came to feel that the quality of listening was very important for the dynamics of classroom thought. It was not just that students needed to listen, they needed to *really listen* and they needed to feel listened to. Classes that "jelled" around this process offered opportunities for emotional interaction that facilitated thought. When students felt safe and listened to, they could risk intellectual exploration. These classes were more interesting for me also, because I too could risk intellectual exploration.

But this presented another demand upon me as a teacher. How could I help develop classes where students really listened? I have come to feel that this goal required two things from me—first, I had to really listen to the students, and second, I had to make sure that any conflicts that developed did not become polarized and ongoing points of struggle. I sought to disrupt any tense conflict by means of questions that neither side to the struggle could answer easily. I tried to avoid taking sides myself in heated discussions. I worked to formulate questions that generated emotional ambivalence, questions that made both sides thoughtful. I am not always able to produce a classroom where people really listen, but I find that the classes that work that way are most satisfying for me and for students.

For most of my career I have had the sense that students are most able to become thoughtful when they are able to "really listen" to a variety of people with different points of view. I became particularly concerned to plan a class discussion that could explore a range of emotional responses. I came to feel that the logical system of ideas that I developed for teaching was less important than I had previously thought. I came to feel that in order to explore logical perspectives on an issue I needed to explore emotional perspectives on an issue. I worked with classes to explore the emotional range of feelings that might respond to an issue.

One award-winning teacher who very self-consciously "works" with the emotional life of his students to promote reflection on and synthesis of potential conflict is Jeffrey Berman. Berman has won many teaching awards and has written many books about his experiences. He has a dedicated following.

One helpful example of the emotional dialectics of classroom interaction comes from Berman's chapter, "Sexual Disclosures," in *Diaries to an English Professor*. A male student has written an entry about a fraternity story he hears from friends. Berman reads this entry aloud to his class:

> A few days ago my friend told me a story about what he and his fraternity brothers did to some innocent, unsuspecting female. While one of their friends was in a room with this girl, they all decided to hide in the closet. After the friend was engaged in coitus with this girl, the fraternity brothers slowly revealed themselves and drew nearer to the bed. They were all naked. When at last she saw them, she struggled to get her clothes on, but her partner for the night held her in the rear-entry position and stayed inside her, until she was finally able to break free and run out of the room. This, as I discovered, was called a "rodeo." It seems that while the girl struggles, the audience would holler out like they were watching a cowboy ride a bull.
>
> Honestly, at first I laughed, I really thought it was funny. I mean, my friends aren't rapists. In fact, the word "rape" didn't come to mind until I thought of all the implications of their actions. This girl was humiliated in front of them, and they loved it. This "rodeo" was purely acting out desires. Just thinking about it now makes me sick. These aren't lowlife degenerates; these were all wealthy, middle-class boys. I guess their drives are just the same as everyone's. But it is hard for me to understand why people need to make someone else suffer in the process. I wish they would have never told me that story. (Berman 1994, 201)

In his last sentence, "I wish they would have never told me that story," the student expresses a desire not to know. Knowledge of the story brings emotional conflict and this conflict foreshadows the possibility of a loss of friends.

The writer begins this story at a point where he, like everyone, has friends who have a range of experiences and talk about them. As the writer enters into this social relationship, the thinking of this group of friends define a limited range of possible thoughts and organize "thought" according to a principle of attachment love. His friends, in his mind, are "not rapists." The word "rapist" isn't quite integrated with the evidence in his mind. It is a word he keeps at arm's length. The emotional body of the student has, all by itself, "chosen" to identify with the friends. They tell him the story. They laugh, and when he hears the story he joins them through an appropriate emotional response. They laugh and he laughs also. The woman is shamed, but her shaming intensifies the bond among the men.

Much later in his career, in a discussion of group psychology, Freud argues that some symptoms develop, somewhat mysteriously, from apparently simple identifications with the behavior of other people. In one often-quoted anecdote Freud describes girls in a boarding school who develop a hysterical cough after one particular girl has such a cough:

> Supposing, for instance, that one of the girls in a boarding school has had a letter from someone with whom she is secretly in love which arouses her jealousy, and that she reacts to it with a fit of hysterics; then some of her friends who know about it will catch the fit, as we say, by mental infection. The mechanism is that of identification based upon the possibility or desire of putting oneself in the same situation. The other girls would like to have a secret love affair too, and under the influence of a sense of guilt they also accept the suffering involved in it. (Freud 1921, 49)

In this example, the symptom is not developed by some personal and private history located in an infantile past. Instead, the symptom is triggered by emotional bonds developed within a group.

Changes in identity are often triggered by emotional and biological responses to social cues. Identity itself is not usually a "thought"; it is an emotional style of being in the world. It is a style developed by interactions with others such that we imitate how others act and think. The emotions of others become emotions we feel within ourselves. Identification is often unconscious, but it typically generates thoughts in the form of words that are organized by feelings lived in the body.

Berman's student, who is forced to respond to the emotional demand of another student, seems caught for a moment within a conflict of attachment. On the one hand, there is an overt attempt to distance himself from his friends, as when the writer says, "It is hard for me to understand why people need to make someone else suffer." And yet the writer is very slow to make a negative judgment of these fraternity boys. "My friends aren't rapists," he says. Perhaps he fears that the same men who shamed this woman would shame him.

A woman in the class who heard the diary entry was able to quickly make the judgment that the male could not make.

> The person who wrote that diary, if I can remember clearly, didn't use the word "rape." Why? In my opinion, that girl was raped in every sense of the word, and what's worse is that a bunch of guys cheered it on! (1994, 202)

We can all recognize the tension that a classroom exchange like this might generate. An entire class will feel, in their own bodies, the drama of a confrontation such as this. Are these "friends" rapists? If this student thinks so, there are consequences. Rapists go to jail. The words that represent thought are caught in a conflict between shame/contempt judgments from different social groups.

The male writer says that he first laughed when he heard the story from a friend. He admits that when he first heard the story, he thought it was funny. His laughter makes him a member of a particular social group that does not make careful observations about harm done to others. One might argue that his laughter is "instinctive" because it reveals how he "really" feels about the event as opposed to what he will say when he is called to speak in front of people who might be uneasy with his friends' "game." Berman's class, however, offers this student different social links, different possibilities for feeling, and thus also different contexts for thought.

Students need to be given freedom to "find themselves" by working through the emotional conflicts of situations such as this. Thinking here, in this moment of emotional tension, is very much caught up in the emotional intensity of attachments. The word "rape" appears when the student thinks with sympathy of the "poor girl" who is the victim of the game. And yet, in this writer's mind, the perpetrators of this game are not rapists, simply because of the fact that they are friends. The meaning of the word "rape" seems determined by the feeling of the word "friend." This structure of thought seems to support Bion's claim that thought follows a logic of love and hate. The writer, caught between thinking about his feeling for the girl and his feeling for his friends, seeks appropriate words. The word "rape" comes to mind when he thinks about the girl, but this word is then banished when he thinks about his friends. This is not logical thought, but it is honest expression. Words reflect the demands placed upon thought by different contexts of emotion. It is an example of how thought has to be "worked through" different contexts of emotion if it is to have any real presence in the mind. The developmental task facing this student is to find himself in relation to the various contexts of experience that the story and its response generates.

What is at stake in how the teacher handles this tension? What are the possibilities and what are the various outcomes? The Joe Sandusky case of 2012 is a useful illustration of how strong emotional attachments pull on the "logic" of moral thought. Joe Paterno, the much beloved and very successful Penn State coach, knew that his assistant, Sandusky, had sexual relations with young boys. There is no other word for this other than rape. Court evidence suggests that Paterno "knew" this was going on, but protected Sandusky from investigation. When Paterno was subjected to intense media scrutiny and widespread blame, he suffered a heart attack and died. His death struck a chord among many fans. Large numbers rallied to support Paterno. Paterno was for them a "good" man.

What made Paterno "good?" Many years of happy and rewarding experience made Joe Paterno loved by his fans. Indeed he did many good things. The Sandusky case, however, asked that Paterno be considered in somewhat different terms. Perhaps Paterno was, in some situations, "not good." The emotional demands of the experience of love are incompatible with the emotional associations of the word "bad." When media attention suggested a need to "think" about Joe Paterno in terms very different from those of years of habitual usage, the demand proved to be very difficult.

Years ago, when I taught a course in argumentation yearly, I would make an assignment where students were asked to write an argument that responded purely to a logic of linguistic meaning, rather than positive or negative value judgments. This kind of argument is termed a CP (Categorical Proposition) argument. For this assignment students were allowed, for example to write an argument like: "George Bush is a moron." But to write a CP argument, which was the student's assignment, such a claim had to be developed through strict, logical, public reference to established linguistic meaning and evidence. A CP claim reasons thus: What is x? According to public use of language, x is defined as y, y being a different and more extensive collection of words or an operational test that defines what x is. For example, if one says, as an argument, "This substance is x (gold)." This substance x can be known to be gold only if it passes a series of careful observations and tests. It is a metal? Is it malleable? Is it yellow? Does it have the chemical character of gold? We can know what x is only if we know if its attributes correspond to its definition.

To argue that George Bush is a moron, one must separate one's feelings from the literal claim of the words. Part of the definition of moron reflects the measurement of an IQ test. At the time I was teaching, a moron was defined as having an IQ of 51–70. George Bush did not have an IQ in this range. Therefore he is not, strictly speaking, a moron. I myself would want to call him a moron. Many people may think of him as stupid or bad, but those kinds of claims make a different kind of argument, a value judgment. Logically, we must recognize the difference between an argument based on fact and an argument developed from a value judgment. It is not logical to insist that George Bush is a moron. And yet I found that though I might repeat this analysis of the CP argument again and again, there were some students who could not take this in.

I found that almost all students had great difficulty writing a CP argument. In early drafts of almost every student, an initial CP claim would tend to drift into a good/bad evaluative argument. Some students could not imagine a CP argument. However hard they tried to start out with a sentence that would formulate a CP claim, their ideas would drift into the form of an evaluative argument. I would talk to them in my office and go through a series of examples, correcting them each time their thinking drifted from a logic of "x is y" to an argument of "x" is bad.

My difficulty in teaching CP argument supports Bion's claim about the causal dynamics driving human thought. Our thought reflects what we love and hate. Even if we try to think about a thing apart from this dynamic, even if our grade depends upon our ability to separate our love and hate from the logical manipulation of language, many of us are unable to maintain the kind of vigilance that allows us to control our "thought." We may recognize the difference between talking about what something is and whether something is good or bad, but however we start out in thinking, our links of ideas go astray. Our minds slip into a characteristic pattern of linking thoughts that reinforce our ideas about what is good and bad.

If Joe Paterno is "good," this verbal claim is not the result of a painstaking evaluative argument in which all sides are considered, the evidence on both sides is weighed, and a most likely generalization formulated. We can see how the reasoning works in this case because, for these fans, not only is Paterno good, but the people who criticized Paterno are "bad." This is an example of the biology of emotion operating upon and speaking through a human being as if the human mind were a machine complying with a demand outside the ability of the mind to process. Love and hate, not reason, control the signifiers that emerge as thought.

Many years ago I gave a talk suggesting that a bad ideology was like a "bad" mother who could not be easily abandoned. After the talk, a professor suggested that making progress in teaching was like reliving the plot of the movie *Groundhog Day*. The plot of *Groundhog Day* revolves around a central character's reliving one particular day over and over again until he is able to find a way to give up his narcissism and establish a relationship to a woman he loves. This professor remarked that every day in class he would dismantle an ideological system, bring his students to this understanding, only to discover the next day that this "dead" ideology was again alive and well and fully operational. It is as if he had to start all over again each class day. This story was told to me in a tone of despair and at the time I was not sure what to make of it, though I was struck with the aptness of its observation.

I would suggest now that this return of the dead ideology is precisely what we must better understand as teachers. We may see, in this return of the dead, a cynical nature of reason and the final irrational nature of symptomatic fixations. It might be more useful to see, in the return of the dead, the insistence of emotion in the expression of thought. We might look upon this "return of the dead" not as the hopelessness of reason, but the expression of reason's core, with which we must engage. The return of the dead is not the sign of failure, but the sign of a necessary process that we must fully embrace. We can most genuinely contribute to thinking if we facilitate this process. We disrupt and attack the process if we simply demand that "proper" thinking be accomplished through following the representation of "logical" thought.

The greatest possibilities for change take place in classrooms that students experience as safe. Classrooms can become social groups that shift people's attachments to people and attachments to the emotional weight of words. One kind of response that I most value in my own teaching evaluations is when students say, "This class became like a family to me." This situation does not happen as frequently as I would like it to, but it generally indicates that students are aware of a variety of different people in the class. These people discuss "difficult" subjects that bring into play conflicting emotions. But these students maintain a certain respect and even develop a measure of love for each other as they explore how they feel and think in relation to a number of charged social issues.

Changes in subjectivity do not take place in a moment of thought. Changes in subjectivity take place in a temporal horizon where a play of thought can have structuring effects on an embodied history of attachment, fear, hope, and security. This prolonged temporal adjustment to new information is, perhaps more than anything else, an exercise in increasing a tolerance for anxiety. Symptomatic fixations hold in place particular relations of language. One cannot simply insist upon a factual truth to change an established network of feeling. Established networks of feeling must be modified if uncomfortable information is to become integrated within an effective mind. The modification of feeling is not sufficiently recognized as an educational task.

CHAPTER FOUR

ACADEMIC ALLEGIANCE AND
ATTACKS ON LINKING

Those of us who teach the required course in literary theory in English or literature departments routinely inform our students of the theory wars of the 1970s and 1980s. For many of us, this time and intellectual context of "war" defined the hope, scope, and purpose of our professional development. In my younger years I felt the "wars" "spearheaded" a new era of intellectual freedom and honesty. (I will signal the problematic phallic thrust of this metaphor with quotation marks. I wish I could signal the emotional dynamic of every word with an inline mark.) Like every war, those of us recruited for service were fighting for "liberation," as I suppose all battles are justified and made righteous.

The theory wars are now often border skirmishes, but they continue, and they continue to define the emotional life of the professional scholar. Every scholar at a conference "takes a position" on historical truth, cultural change, or literary interpretation. Participants express their arguments and support their position in relation to opposing points of view. We all develop in a culture where the "strength" of an intellectual is expressed in her ability to "win" arguments and silence opponents. All of us, professionals in the service of various positions, publish papers and establish our prestige and importance in relation to an only slightly sublimated framework of war: ideas we defeat and ideas we advance.

I worry that the skills we are most required to develop as professional educators make us unprepared for and inattentive to the teaching that develops flexible and integrated minds. When success becomes measured by defeating the enemy, skills in synthesis of uncomfortable and conflicted information become subordinated to victory over opposing ideas. Teachers often win arguments by silencing their oppositional students. But oppression is not persuasion.

If we want to develop a healthy and responsible society, we must understand how our emotional commitment to the metaphor of war and mastery defeats our ability to develop flexible thought. To solve problems, we must integrate new and uncomfortable information. Learning to be nondefensive in the assimilation of new information is as important as insistence on logical rigor. Few academics, however, can afford the gestures of nondefensive thought—long pauses in thought, reversals in position—in debate.

Our profession insists upon mastery, and this insistence polices idealized practices of thought with regrettable results. "Work" in the humanities should develop minds resilient in the emotional assimilation of new information. Many teachers in small classrooms implicitly understand this process. Good teachers intuitively interact productively, rather than negatively, with the emotions of their students. In many departments, however, the ethos of the "teacher" is in conflict with the ethos of the successful publishing scholar.

Emotional Growth and the Liberal Arts Tradition

There has been a tradition in the liberal arts devoted to the growth of the mind. In 1916, John Dewey argued that a liberal arts education contributed to the growth of the mind and prepared it for participation in democratic society. These ideas were not entirely new when John Dewey wrote, and they are now generally familiar to most of us. They were embraced with particular enthusiasm during World War II and again during the Cold War when Western values were characterized as democratic in sharp contrast to the authoritarian values of Germany and later Russia. Educators found it useful to emphasize that democracy developed through a particularly Western liberal arts tradition, and politicians have generally been happy to publicly support this claim. More recently, the liberal arts tradition has been questioned by both the entrepreneurial values of the political Right and the Foucauldian critique of liberal knowledge on the academic Left.

Despite its embattled position, the liberal arts model continues to have credibility. Most accounts of the "growth" of the mind have given emphasis to the creative dimensions of the liberal arts experience. On its website the Association of American Colleges and Universities defines the rewards of a liberal arts education in the following manner:

> A truly liberal education is one that prepares us to live responsible, productive, and creative lives in a dramatically changing world. It is an education that fosters a well-grounded intellectual resilience, a disposition toward lifelong learning, and an acceptance of responsibility for the ethical consequences of our ideas and actions. Liberal education requires that we understand the foundations of knowledge and inquiry about nature, culture and society; that we master core skills of perception, analysis, and expression; that we cultivate a respect for truth; that we recognize the importance of historical and cultural context; and that we explore connections among formal learning, citizenship, and service to our communities. ("Statement on Liberal Learning")

This creed gives emphasis to many admirable qualities that purportedly follow from a liberal arts training—"intellectual resilience," "respect for truth," and commitment to "life long learning." Many educators support these claims intuitively, but it has been hard to prove that these changes in fact take place. And it has been hard to describe how these changes take place.

I propose that we can understand the growth of the mind as a function of learning to tolerate painful emotions related to an uncomfortable thought. The desire not to know is particularly intense when we must face information that undermines our sense of security. Uncomfortable information directly impacts our emotional life. It requires that we think and "hold" in our minds ideas that create anxiety or anger. Often uncomfortable information triggers barely tolerable emotions such as shame and rage. In the earlier chapters I described classroom interactions where shame, contempt, and anger threaten to shut down possibilities for curiosity and reflection. Emotional growth requires the ability to "manage" the power of these emotions. Management means not the denial, suppression, or dismissal of such emotions but their integration within more complex networks of thought and feeling. How does this happen? How can we describe the emotional "work" of mind?

Traditional descriptions of liberal arts practices describe student-teacher interactions. Small classrooms with engaged discussions are good. Relaxed engagement with smart personable professors is enlivening. Fully engaged Socratic dialogues contribute to alert, flexible thinking. But we can be more specific in describing emotional exercises that grow the mind.

Arthur Frank, a sociologist, writes about the need for life-narrative revision in response to the hard truths of illness. Illness, he observes, demands that we accept what seems at the same time both true and impossible to bear. Illness requires the acceptance of uncomfortable information. Illness entails a loss of function, a loss of the capacity to work, a loss often of friends and meaningful activities. Frank insists that coping with these losses demands narrative revisions that, as he says, do "emotional work." Medical research supports findings that indicate that the "emotional work" of revised life narratives reduce stress and contribute to the mental and physical health of the writer (Ray 2004).

Frank's account of the "emotional work" of writing the illness narrative describes the "emotional work" of taking in uncomfortable information. Like the truth of illness, new and uncomfortable information often demands changes in the knower's life. Just as people with illness must cope with the loss of friends, loss of an imagined future, and loss of an established frame of security, so also the implications of new information can mean very similar losses. Frank argues that emotional work requires having the courage to face fear. "Naming is crucial," Frank says. "The fears that are most insidious are those that cannot be named and thus cannot be spoken. Fears multiply in silence" (2007, 388).

This analysis of facing fear may be helpful for understanding crucial emotional dynamics in the successful liberal arts classroom. In an earlier chapter I offered various stories of the desire not to know. In all these stories knowing is experienced as a threat. Knowing can entail a loss of friends, loss of an imagined future, and a loss of established frames of emotional security. The fear that attends illness is usually more intense, conscious, and constant than the fears of thinking a new thought. Nonetheless, new thoughts often do introduce a fear that goes unnoticed when we image the mind as a machine adapted for thought.

Consider the examples for the earlier chapters that represent moments of integrated knowing. In all these cases, fear threatens the thinker, and the thinker denies a problem solving thought, by not integrating fearful but important information. Norman Mailer's Sergeant Martinez rejects "knowing" the lie he has told. To face the fact would mean losing the support of First Sergeant Croft and losing his own prestige as a soldier. Knowing is too costly for him. So also J. G. Farrell's Japanese foot soldier Kikuchi cannot "know" his own thoughts about the recklessness of Lieutenant Matsusita, even though his desire not to know Matsusita may result in his own death. The threat of death is preferable to the loss of an established frame of belief defined by country and military values. So also with Gilman Perkins's imprisoned wife in the short story "The Yellow Wallpaper." Her imagination moves her to question her husband's wisdom. Her thinking reaches a point where she is able to formulate the interior thought, "What is one to do?" But at that point, the possibility of something to do might be real, such as question her husband's judgment. She can go no further in her thinking. We might posit that this woman fears the loss of her husband. In all these stories the courage to think requires the courage to face and suffer loss. Thought ends precisely at a point where fear becomes palpable.

In Jeffrey Berman's English class the student who makes the claim that his friends are "not rapists" faces a similar crisis. If he says that his friends are rapists, he faces the potential loss of these friends. A woman in the class, however, pushes this student to take the next step in thought. Much depends, I would argue, on how the emotional mood of the classroom gives this student space for honest reflection. Can this moment exercise "emotional work"? Can this moment offer this student the courage to face his fears? How might we describe classrooms that support this work?

A drama emerges in the class the moment the woman in the class accuses the man's friends of rape. Moments of accusation such as these are very tense moments. They are precisely the kind of moments liberal educators need to understand. This is precisely a moment when new knowledge requires nondefensive thought. The shift between one perspective and its supporting feelings to another perspective with new implications and new emotions to be "sorted through" is characteristically a time of some disorientation, and, at best, reverie. We feel vulnerable because we have lost something we had felt was secure.

The emotional life of our immediate social context is very important in this moment of transition. Some groups respect and idealize the courage of personal honesty. Some social groups, requiring unambivalent commitment, have no sympathy for moments of ambivalence that might lead to changes in belief. Ambivalence undermines commitment, and can therefore threaten to undermine "truth" itself. In such cases contempt polices any ambivalence that might lead to internal reorganization.

As academics are trained for the warfare of ideas, and may be committed to the various truths of the profession, they may have no sympathy for ambivalence and nondefensive thought. Rather than seeking to find space and support for such moments of thought, they may seek to show contempt or disapproval for such moments. In this manner they impair the life of reason. The idealization of professional mastery, to the extent that it demands full conviction and vilifies hesitation, disorientation, and ambivalent silence, idealizes the desire not to know. The life of reason is thus undermined by the very professionalism that ostensibly supports it.

The Metaphor of War in the Academic Community

Academic communities are organized much as any other human community. Shared values and beliefs organize the community. Ideas that threaten established group beliefs are attacked. What often seem most visible in academic disputes are the verbal arguments formulated. What is often less visible is the basis of emotional dynamics of the response—shame, anger, dismissal, contempt.

I cannot speak for all academics, but I can speak from my own location in the humanities. My training was very heavily in literary theory. The "theory wars" were intensely fought debates in literary theory from the 1960s to the 1980s. Radical new ideas about language and representation, developed largely in France, had an impact originally in elite centers such as Yale, Johns Hopkins, and Cornell, and spread outward to the rest of the country. Just as formalism radically changed methods for literary study in the 1930s and 1940s, reader-response, post-structuralism, deconstruction, and cultural studies radically changed frameworks for thinking about literature in the 1970s and 1980s. Anyone who majors in English is trained within the framework of these "theory wars." Professor Arnie Sanders at Goucher College introduces his course in Critical Methods by offering some background:

While the "Theory Wars" raged, scholars in our discipline were willing to destroy each other, socially and professionally, for the sake of ideas they held so dear that no price was too high to pay in order to advance them. The public, political consequences of some theories arguably have led to the deaths of millions, and the battles within English Departments have resulted in the firings of both senior and junior faculty, and even produced at least one formal challenge to a duel of honor in a state institution very near Maryland. These powerful ideas have made and broken careers, and have resulted in the emergence of a set of "celebrity" scholars. ("English 215: Critical Methods")

This context of an ongoing academic "war" is one where a developing academic forms her identity by the exercise of a skill. In this context of "war," at least two sides seek to advance their territory. They look for points of vulnerability, devise strategic attacks, and deliver crushing blows to their opponents. Professors teach with the implicit understanding that their position is in opposition to other thinkers in other theoretical frameworks.

A key assumption of the theory wars is that the bad guys, the people with dangerous ideas, will win if "we," the good guys, are not vigilant, rigorous, and forceful. The English department at Goucher College gives its incoming English majors an overview of the "war" into which they will enter:

> This is the scholarly world you find yourself joining. No one can tell whether the Theory Wars really are over, or merely in a temporary "truce." The most promising/threatening source of new theoretical activism comes from the American Neo-Conservative movement. As recently as the 1990s, English Departments in Ivy League institutions experienced a spate of "revenge" attacks in which politically Liberal or Radical Leftist scholars who had triumphed in the 1970s and '80s suddenly found themselves under attack by scholars energized by the "New Conservatism" that was announced by backers of Ronald Reagan and Newt Gingrich. These conservative scholars continue to have strong political backing and research funding via conservative "think tanks" and lobbying organizations, and they tend to specialize in revisionist literary history of the 1960s–1980s which depicts the reaction against New Criticism as something akin to a Communist plot to take over the universities. Unable to command respect in or to tolerate the practices they saw in the Modern Language Association and other ruling bodies governing the

practices of literary scholarship, they have created their own parallel and hostile bodies, the "Association of Literary Scholars and Critics" and the more broadly-focused "National Association of Scholars," with parallel conventions, publications, conferences, funding channels (The American Enterprise Institute, and the Hoover Institution at Stanford U.), etc. If you find English 215's approach to critical methods too "leftist," I encourage you to research scholars working with these groups, though I must admit I have no sympathy for most of their basic assumptions. If you think the battles of Movement politics are over and the "good guys/gals" won, I also urge you to challenge your complaisant theoretical position by checking out the opposition and its funding. (Sanders, "Critical Methods and the 20th Century's 'Theory Wars'")

The web page alerts students to the "world at war" they enter as English majors: "This is the scholarly world you find yourself joining. No one can tell whether the Theory Wars really are over, or merely in a temporary 'truce.'" Just as Goucher College suggests that perhaps the "good guys" won, but cannot rest from their labors, all professors understand that if they are not vigilant the "enemy" will advance.

The theory wars, of course, are wars of words. We develop precise and nuanced verbal attention as part of our rigorous training as academics. We make advances in the "war" when the words that our side uses to understand an event are adopted and repeated by new recruits. Our success is our ability to spread our beliefs. Unlike literal war, where territory won is marked by the dead bodies of the defenders, academic wars are won by the increased spread of ideas. The spread of ideas is recognized in ever-expanded circles of scholarly publication. Victorious battlefields are defined by the perception of "dead ideas."

The history of the "theory wars" is littered with the corpses of dead ideas. Many of the ideas of literary training that were sacrosanct in my early years of literary training are now "dead" ideas. Classic formalist beliefs are now "dead." Post-structuralist ideas, which largely killed formalist concepts, are showing weaknesses. New literary history and cultural studies has marshalled forth arguments that subject scholars thinking false ideas to shame. All of us who join the theory wars are aware that if we are not muscular in our professional practice, our ideas also will be "dead." Marxists check the indexes of new publications to see how and where Marx is quoted and Lacanians check the indexes to see how and where Lacan quoted. If there is a falling off of citations, one is losing the "war."

In many ways the real and ritualized combat of the theory wars resemble the real and ritualized combat of the fourteenth-century Crusades. True ideas are at war with "false beliefs." Wars are fought over books and their interpretation. Large expanses of territory can be won or lost. Leaders build their reputation in terms of territory won. Leadership is established by preaching and writing, but also, most dramatically by "jousting" at regional gatherings of knights. When conference presenters are distinguished scholars, there is ceremony and pageantry involved in the ritual of the academic presentation as knightly jousts. Strong scholars are recognized in highly ritualized and ceremonial forms of address. Displays of finely crafted language alert everyone to the prestige, lineage, and power of a visitor's participation.

Our pageantry is in our diction and forms of recognition. There is also much ceremony in the battle of words itself. Words are weapons with distinctive features. We deliver the "blows" of combat in a carefully chosen, appropriately timed, and elegantly delivered performance. There are various elaborately classified assertions, ripostes, and innuendos. An initial paragraph can set up a ceremonial confrontation between opposing "warriors." Like the sword and the lance, smartly chosen words can deliver "fatal" or "wounding" strikes in academic combat. A carefully constructed sentence can be decisive in destroying the position of the opposing party and many scholars come home from a conference exulting in their verbal success or still suffering the wounds that define their losses. Conference presentations are places where professionals "advance" their ideas. A scholar presents a paper to promote a particular understanding, and the achievement of this understanding is one small advance in a war of ideas.

What is at stake is the truth of belief. Defending one's own belief, as in the religious wars of the Middle Ages, is a very serious matter. As words are our weapons in the business of war, their use is elaborately coded and fetishized.

The presentation of scholarly papers has a performative aspect akin to the pageantry and jousting of medieval knights. When scholars prepare for conference presentations, they gather their symbols of heraldry. They testify to their lineage. They exhibit particular styles of verbal combat. Words are power. A warrior knows their reach and scope.

We are trained in graduate programs where differently positioned professors commonly compete with each other in their ability to effectively reproduce their ideas. Key to the repetition of ideas is the repetition of words—theoretical concepts and frames of understanding. In literature departments there are experts devoted to various "proper" frames for understanding artistic and historical production—historical understanding, cultural critique, and a few formalists seeking to instruct students in the proper way of thinking. Students come into our programs needing to "define themselves" in relation to their professional identity. Defining oneself means finding a theoretical framework where you are comfortable and then reproducing that framework in your own writing and personal alliances. Typically defining yourself means promoting your group's ideas in relation to other ideas that are faulty, incomplete, or foolish. We identify with the truth of our own group. We promote the truth of that group. We receive satisfaction and validation through the conversion of others to our own ideas. We are admired and rewarded by our superiors for our dedication to the cause.

I am writing from the perspective of an academic humanist with 40 years of professional experience. I am not competent to describe the community of science. Perhaps scholars in the sciences are more immediately responsive to the immediacy of evidence. But science is also made of communities motivated by paradigms, agendas, alliances, and urgent demands. Edward O. Wilson, for example, argues that the human impulse to use technology has been consistently motivated by the metaphor of war:

> Throughout history, the escalation of large part of technology has had combat as its central purpose. Today, the calendars of nations are punctuated by holidays to celebrate wars won and to perform memorial services for those who died waging them. Public support is best fired up by appeal to the emotions of deadly combat over which the amygdala is grandmaster. (2012, 62)

Academic communities are perhaps like all human communities in that they organize themselves in response to a sense of urgency and vitality that enlivens the meaning of what they think.

I do not propose that the "metaphor" of war turns us all into mindless empire builders. I also do not believe that we can simply "choose" other more rational patterns of behavior. Human motivation is more complicated that these imaginary choices between war and a rationality. The lived drama of urgent human motivation is always war. This is our inherited biological equipment of the fight or flight response in our reptilian brain. We can become better at avoiding war, but cannot "choose" to avoid the organizing drama and trauma of the war metaphor.

I would like to imagine that we could have more control over our organizational motives. But I have seen many academic organizations opposed to violence fall prey to the violence of factional divisions. I have seen myself and others helpless in the face of issues that bitterly divide an organization. Division over belief quickly shades into hostile human relations, even among people who are gentle, sophisticated about the operations of the mind, and critical of such relations.

This transition from gentle, sophisticated intellectualism to hostile human relations is what I want to examine here. In the discussion that follows I will describe one particular presentation given at a conference in 2010. I knew most of the people involved very well. I saw a presentation that might have generated thoughtful reflection create what Wilson terms "amygdala" alarm. The story of this presentation very powerfully illustrates links between reason and emotion. It illustrates, as well, an attack on reason itself by a swiftly mobilized rhetoric of war.

Emotional Dynamics in the Academic Presentation: A Case Study

On March 3, 2010, Professor Charles "Fred" Alford presented a thoughtful paper in a national trauma conference held at Washington, DC. Professor Alford's paper was on the trauma of Holocaust victims. Professor Alford is Professor and Distinguished Scholar Teacher at the University of Maryland. He is the author of 16 books published by leading presses, some of the most recent being *Narrative, Nature and the Natural Law: From Aquinas to International Rights* (2010); *After the Holocaust: The Book of Job, Primo Levi, and the Journey to Affliction* (2009); and *Psychology and the Natural Law of Reparation* (2006).

Professor Alford gave a very interesting and thoughtful talk, but what was most interesting about the talk, for my purposes here, was the fact that he was not allowed to finish. Although the conference organizers had assigned an entire panel time for Professor Alford alone to deliver his paper, he had such urgent and angry interruptions he stopped to respond to his critics. Professor Alford's ideas were perceived as "dangerous." When he stopped to listen, he became more vulnerable to attack. He was "besieged" as he responded to intense and increasingly hostile questions. Witnesses to the presentation on both sides observed that the word that was repeated most often in the discussion was the word "attack." Both sides to the discussion experienced themselves under attack. The body language in response to the presentation was strongly suggestive of a physical attack. And each person present was a well-intentioned, sophisticated academic or clinician normally horrified at any thought of overt physical intimidation.

My purpose in this description of the Alford presentation is not to blame either side for stupidity, aggression, or obstinate bullheadedness. My purpose is to show how established rituals of scholarly practice draw genuinely thoughtful people into combat. The ritual of the scholarly presentation structures interpersonal relations such that encounters with new information are experienced as an attack.

The title of Professor Alford's talk was "Was the Holocaust Traumatic?" An abstract that summed up his argument follows:

> One of the most influential contemporary accounts of psychological trauma, that of Cathy Caruth and the neurobiologists she draws on, does not fit some of the most traumatized men and women of the twentieth century: survivors of the Holocaust. Should this lead us to rethink trauma theory, or would we instead decide that the Holocaust is a special case? In making my argument, I draw upon my research in the Fortunoff Video Archives for Holocaust Testimony at Yale University. It is primarily from these testimonies that my examples of accounts of trauma are drawn, accounts that don't fit either Caruth's theory, or the way most think about Post Traumatic Stress Disorder (PTSD). Often it is more useful to view trauma from a phenomenological or experiential perspective, one that looks at psychological trauma from the perspective of the traumatized. This view accounts for the historical context within which trauma takes place without turning PTSD into a driving force of history. (Fred Alford, Feb. 22, 2010, email to author)

The intent of the argument seems straightforward. Professor Alford spent considerable time with the Yale Fortunoff Video Archives, paying careful attention to the people interviewed and their stories. After viewing the tapes and pondering the issues involved, he came to believe that a particular dominant academic understanding of trauma (one that "understands" trauma as "unrepresentable") was an obstacle to taking in an important message from the archives.

Most scholars are trained in the formal procedures that "in theory" can quickly cool down an "overheated" argument. One virtue of argumentation theory is its insistence that belief should never float free of evidence. If a person makes an argument, but the only support for such an argument is simply another argument, then such an argument has no possibility of persuading a person not already persuaded. No amount of repetition, insistence, emphasis, or intimidation leads to persuasion. Persuasion requires that a person unsure of a truth claim take in credible information. Only credible information can shift a person's evaluations of an issue.

This principle has a useful corollary. A rational person can always in any dispute—no matter how heated—ask about the concrete particulars regarding the evidence supporting an argument. If, for example, Alford says that Fortunoff interviewee Goldberg narrated his story with appropriate affect, an opponent can ask how many years after the Holocaust the interview took place. Normally requests for clarification are not experienced as attacks. Clarification is not direct confrontation; it generally calms people locked in dispute. If there is a trained and experienced facilitator in the group, a third and neutral party, this facilitator can easily find a framework to call both sides to some order. The facilitator can reorganize the discussion and establish an even give and take of ideas focusing on the shared question of creditable evidence. In the case of Fred Alford's presentation, I was the facilitator. I experienced myself as sympathetic to both sides. I knew most people involved quite well. I had, in addition to the facts about the principles of argumentation, some skill in managing heated debates. I could not, however, find a way to manage the emotions of the presentation.

Like most scholars, Professor Alford developed his claims in opposition to dominant ideas. The scholar most associated with the claim that trauma is "unrepresentable" is Professor Cathy Caruth (1996). Professor Caruth was present at the conference but not during Professor Alford's presentation. Some of the discomfort generated by the talk reflected the feelings of people loyal to the ideas of Professor Caruth. But the most intense discomfort generated by the talk came from a second community of people.

Fred's presentation (I shift to a first name attempting to represent the personal immediacy of the talk) took place in the same room where, earlier, there was a panel that had been devoted to understanding Holocaust survivors. Many of the presenters and members of the audience who had attended the earlier talk stayed back for Fred's talk. I think it must have been true that the previous talk had been a very satisfying experience for the presenters and for the people in the audience. Many of the individuals present were psychoanalysts and some of them had parents who had survived the Holocaust camps. This group had bonded through the previous presentations. The previous talk had helped them recognize and honor the memory of their parents. The previous talk also gave them a fitting language to frame and understand these events. The word "trauma" attached to the words "Holocaust survivor" had been experienced as a significant truth.

Fred's argument that many survivors did not have PTSD was delivered in the classic form of a "provocative" academic paper. A "provocative" paper has a particular rhetoric that very cleanly formulates an original and unexpected argument and then supports that argument through an elegant array of supporting observations. Provocative papers are very effective appeals to thought. They are very difficult to dismiss. Provocative papers can pull readers roughly into thinking a chaotic mix of ideational claims.

The presentation quickly became an intense struggle over truth claims. As people tried to offer evidence to support their positions, the presentation of evidence itself seemed to intensify the hostility of the encounter. Claims regarding evidence were experienced as body blows. These blows were given and returned by very smart people able to quickly recognize vulnerable positions, remember information, and defend themselves with the verbal equivalents of effective upper jabs, kidney punches, and strong roundhouse connections.

The challenge presented by Fred's presentation was one that involved the appropriate choice of concepts. What concept best describes these people in the archives who narrate their experiences of the Holocaust? Did Sidney Green (let us call him) demonstrate an ability to "narrate traumatic events?" Or did Mr. Green's narration indicate his capture by an "unrepresentable" trauma. Thinking about this question would not seem to require a title match.

As I sit here in my study on a calm, Sunday afternoon this problem of choosing the most useful concept seems eminently manageable. One simply discriminates carefully among useful concepts. Is the behavior these people show the behavior of PTSD? Is it not PTSD? One reviews the evidence. One describes the behavior carefully. One reviews the concept's definition. One matches the right concept with the evidence.

The talk, from this perspective, might seem to require a simple act of judgment. But if you had been present in the same room on that particular day with that particular group of people, you would have found it very difficult to escape the impassioned call for defense or attack. I find it curious that I have, as a writer of a standard academic text, almost no resources to represent that room. I can say that the people were very angry. But when I write a sentence like that, I do not bring to your embodied thought the intensity of "raw" emotion in the room. I am not able to make the feeling present to you, right now, as a reader. If, right now, you were to look up from this book and see someone striking your window with an axe, your reaction might resemble the quality of the emotion generated in that room then. If you then imagine yourself confronting the man with the axe and discover him yelling at you, you might begin to imagine the emotional quality of that room. Somehow a simple act of judgment became saturated with a feeling of physical combat.

Any thought present in the room seemed so wedded to an impulsive sense of threat that sentences exchanged between various parties were registered only in terms of raw fear and defense.

How did this happen?

It is a struggle to find any language for representing the possible cause of this event, but what perhaps comes most close is to suggest that Fred's argument was experienced by his opposition as an act of desecration. It was as if they had mothers and fathers killed by the Holocaust. They had just enjoyed a panel where their parents were given honor and dignity for their sacrifice. And then Fred came and urinated on the graves of those parents.

Of course Fred did not do any such thing. He did nothing even close to that act. But at that time and place Fred's language, his argument that the Holocaust survivors were not suffering from PTSD, was tantamount to desecration. Let me be more explicit. I am asserting that in particular conditions, for many academics, a particular arrangement of signifiers, an arrangement largely meaningless for the lay public, that is, "The Holocaust survivors were not suffering from PTSD," is the emotional equivalent of a hate crime.

Human beings can become quickly bonded to human language, creating conditions where threats to words acquire deep links to very primitive regions of the brain. It is as if an amygdala fight or flight response was called into play by a simple shift in concepts.

I met with Fred and one of his colleagues afterward. This friend had arrived late and discovered an enraged group of people. He was incredulous. He expressed disbelief that the talk could have generated such opposition and hostility. How could something like this happen?

This disbelief was echoed by other participants. Jean Wyatt wrote me shortly after the conference and remarked on the response to Fred's presentation:

> I was in the audience for the first 45 minutes of Fred's presentation, thinking that what Fred was saying was interesting and certainly inoffensive, and was amazed at the rage of the people in the audience. I had to leave to go to dinner with... at 6, but... said that the rage went on for the whole time. Do you understand why people were so furious?

Jean says she was "amazed" at the audience response. I talked with Esther Rashkin after the talk also and she used similar language. She was "just amazed at the hostility" generated. This kind of wonder in witnessing the emotional responses to the presentation sounds very much like Ramachandran's comment about his anosognosia patient. We see human beings talking. Their minds are producing speech, but the linking of idea to idea is so outside the realm of what minds are supposed to exhibit as "thought" that we cannot "believe" what we hear.

The "disbelief" we feel testifies to a "belief" in reason. We follow very insistent internal feelings that academic speech expresses the "force" of reason. Fred's presentation clearly called into play a different "force" driving speech. We see this dynamic working. But it is unbelievable. We seem unable to connect our understanding of what we see happening with our understanding of what a mind does. We cannot image a brain so powerfully held hostage by a primitive biology. People who witnessed Fred's talk responded much as Ramachandran had when he saw his patient insist that her right arm works. It clearly does not work; it clearly lies lifeless by her side.

As academics, we have committed our lives to the principle of reason and when we see this principle as having no force, we cannot shift into another understanding of what generates verbal statements. When we cannot imagine these conditions, we cannot fully think about them. We thus cannot grasp what is going on in our own inner life.

Bion argues that verbal production is an expression of emotional loves and hates. This emotional force behind speech does not follow the assumptions of reason and logic and will not respond to the principles of reason and logic. Fred's presentation illustrates this claim. Fred had argued, and later repeated in an email to me that "Holocaust survivors are in general traumatized, but that PTSD does not work as a description of their trauma." This claim was experienced as insufferable. It was imperative that Fred had to be stopped.

Donald Meltzer writes that a "new idea" presents itself as an "emotional experience" (1988, 20). In describing new ideas as "emotional experience," Meltzer rephrases Stanley Fish's claim. Thought is not a response to evidence but a bias toward evidence. Academics tend to consider ideas as emotionally denuded—signifiers, representations, cognitive codes. We hear our colleagues talk and we characteristically hear meanings (not feelings) we support or attack. We pretend as if emotion plays no role in defending or attacking. But even when academics believe they follow simple logic in their linked thoughts, they often follow the logic of Bion's emotional algebra. Thoughts are linked by the associational logic of love or hate.

Fred's presentation quickly energized a large room with raw emotion. I was very interested in the experience of the presentation and I knew at the time that I wanted to write about it. I wrote to see if I could find out more about Fred's experience. He wrote back quickly.

In my email I had compared the audience response as an attachment to what rhetorician Kenneth Burke described as "god terms." Burke argued that just as people defended their faith to the death during the Middle Ages as God's truth, so any tightly organized group will defend belief. (Burke 1950).

My guess is that Fred offended the God terms of three different groups of scholars. Some were more offended than others, but the interaction of the three created and amplified a scene of intense frustration and anger. The angriest were the people offended by the idea that PTSD did not describe Holocaust survivors.

In his email to me afterward, Fred summed up three points he wanted to make about the PTSD diagnosis. Fred was focusing upon the ideational content of the interaction. I will be presenting, though, two emails from Fred. The first email represents Fred's first response to the disruptive presentation. It shows Fred engaged in a largely cognitive framework of reflection. A second email, to which I will give more attention, reveals Fred's report of the emotional experience of the interaction. I will review and comment on both emails. Here is the first:

1. My goal was to say that yes, Holocaust survivors are in general traumatized, but that PTSD does not work as a description of their trauma, for they can narrate their trauma well; doing so just doesn't help.
2. Even while a wider, more descriptive characterization of trauma, what I called a phenomenological view, accurately captures the experience of most survivors, this is still not a good way to look at survivors.
3. The whole problem is that of seeing survivors as survivors. We should see them as our teachers. (Fred Alford, email to author, March 11, 2010)

When Fred suggests that we think of these survivors as "teachers "rather than PTSD victims," he is offering improved concepts for thinking about the survivors. Talking about survivors as teachers might have been a useful reframing of terms during the talk.

A second group of people offended by Fred were scholars loyal to the work on trauma by Cathy Caruth. Fred summed up his argument on this issue afterward:

4. The lit. critters on trauma, like Caruth, understand that trauma is historical, but they are so concerned with its non-representable content that they lose the perspective of the Holocaust survivor as teacher about an objective (and objectively evil) world. For the

lit critters, trauma has taken the place of Yahweh, the G_d who cannot be named.

Fred here represents the heart of the disagreement. In representing the "lit. critters" thus, he signals his recognition of the limits of their possibilities for dialogue in that particular event. The talk was not experienced as an exercise in thought, but as a violation of religious truth. The word "trauma," Fred claims, has "taken the place of Yahweh."

A third point of contention for Fred was the psychiatric reports on trauma survivors. He summed up his point on this issue:

> 5. The psychiatrists are so confined to the consulting room that they can hardly imagine the relevance or importance of seeing the survivor as someone with a lesson to teach us—and not primarily as someone who needs to be healed.
> 6. In terms of your (anti) trauma God, the lit critters see non-representation as their God. The psychiatrists see what happens in the consulting room, healing the victim, as their God.

These six points represent the key claims of the talk. Fred proposes a different way of "seeing" trauma and his opponents worry that this shift in perspective threatens sacred values.

The room was full of scholars who were experts in their field. I had hoped for a good discussion. In the audience were two former Yale Medical School professors and psychiatrists, Doctors Art Blank and Harold Kudler who had worked to define PTSD and continue to work with trauma patients. They bring to their thinking many decades of reflection, wide experience with patients, and passionate engagement in the issues. When Fred saw one of these men shaking his head violently, he stopped his talk.

The audience had been asked to follow the sequence of claims in Fred's talk and respond thoughtfully. Much evidence suggests that Fred's argument was eminently thinkable. Jean Wyatt followed it with interest. We term a good talk "thoughtful" because it leaves us with significant thought. At the time of the talk, few people in the room would have termed the talk thoughtful. But good evidence for the thoughtfulness of the presentation came later from an audience member, Dr. Blank, who was irritated by the talk at the time.

Dr. Blank was a member of the audience when the talk was given. He was sitting next to a friend, Dr. Harold Kudler, and initially his responses to Fred sided with most of the audience. He had spent a great deal of time working with trauma patients and disagreed firmly with some of the claims Fred was making. Six months later I asked Fred to present his talk, somewhat revised, at a trauma seminar I ran at George Washington University. I asked Dr. Blank to comment on the paper and his response was thoughtful, still in disagreement, but supportive of the paper's provocative gesture. He wrote, "A marvellous and stimulating paper" (Art Blank, email to author, Nov. 11 2010). The email defined Dr. Blank's orientation toward what later became an interesting study group discussion organized around Fred's paper. Dr. Blank found Fred's slightly revised paper thoughtful. This "thoughtfulness" could have taken place at the conference. Why did it not take place?

To what extent should academics be responsible for managing the emotional contexts of academic experiences? Can we be trained to better manage such experiences? Would such training, in fact, improve the entire discipline of the humanities? I think it would.

Emotional Contexts and Traumatized Social Groups

The emotional dynamics of the group intensified the difficulty of the ideas presented. Damasio argues that particular emotional contexts determine what is remembered and what is not remembered. If ideal liberal arts classrooms offer ideal opportunities for the emotional assimilation of knowledge and Fred Alford's conference event represents the failure of thought, it behooves us as a profession to consider how presentations go wrong, and how commonplace assumptions about scholarly thought betray possibilities for thought.

Somewhere between the March presentation of the paper and the October revision of the paper, Fred Alford, the presenter, and Art Blank, an audience member, became "thoughtful" about the ideas. I think it is fair to say that both people had worked to think their way to a better interaction of thought. Fred revised some sentences to make ideas more easy to assimilate. Most importantly, Dr. Blank had the chance to read Fred's paper on his own, apart from the intense emotion of the presentation room.

Dr. Blank had many objections to Fred's argument. He wrote:

Page 4: pgh 1:...unable to testify in a coherent manner...It is not accurate to generalize about "the traumatized" and "the victim"— Persons exposed to extreme trauma vary widely in the psychopathological effects which they show, and vary widely in the extent to which they can think and speak a coherent historical narrative of their experiences. At one end is total amnesia for events, sometimes accompanied by dissociated re-living actions. At the other end are persons with little PTSD symptoms who are able to coherently narrate their experiences soon after they occurred. In the instance of the Holocaust, there are millions of people distributed along this continuum. (Email to author, Nov. 11, 2010)

Dr. Blank is not in agreement with Fred Alford, but he is comfortable with his disagreements. Effective scholars, I would argue, are generally not anxious in relation to disagreements. Disagreements can often be enlivening. The task for teachers is to understand how disagreements that can become anxious and embattled are shifted into more congenial emotional interactions.

I went to Fred's presentation anticipating an emotionally stirred up audience. I had prepared a statement that I anticipated could lower the intensity of the emotion and introduce reflective thought. On the day before the presentation, I had written a few sentences that I hoped might offer a context to "think" Fred's claim. I was seeking to formulate questions that would shift the demand for thinking to a reorienting point of reference that was neither Fred's argument, nor the argument of the various oppositions. One sentence I had written was, "Trauma has a history, it harms people, and it is our moral responsibility to understand it even if the attempt at understanding is difficult and unsettling and violating of near sacred boundaries." This record shows that I had anticipated the very event that happened. I had anticipated an event of the violations of "near sacred boundaries." I had captured neatly in concepts what took place. But my conceptual anticipation did not provide me with a real imaginative grasp of what happened. My concepts, while accurate, failed to grasp the real experience of what transpired.

I was prepared for the debate. I had written out many sentences beforehand to use in focusing the discussion. I was using a strategy that often works for me as a teacher. I verbally represented the fears people had about the presentation. I sought to give them thoughtful attention. But I could not find a place in the engagement where any of these ideas could effectively "connect."

William Cronon argues, "A liberal education is about gaining the power and the wisdom, the generosity and the freedom to connect" (1998, 79). Connecting, it seems to Cronon, is a "power" allied to "wisdom." Further, he claims it to be facilitated by "generosity" and "freedom." I think it is important, first, that Cronon uses emotional language to describe the work of connecting, and, second, that this language appeals to intuitions about emotion and learning that are difficult to represent in sharp logical formulas.

Many people believe that "dangerous" ideas should not circulate and contaminate other people. During the presentation a few people said this explicitly. On both sides of the argument, the stakes were high. Both sides wanted to avoid another Holocaust. The ideals of both sides were admirable. And each side saw the other side as promoting dangerous thought. Professor Alford felt that we could only learn about the Holocaust if we accept the survivors as people who could narrate their experiences with accuracy and integrity. On the other hand, people felt that if one imagines a survivor as someone lacking the dignity of traumatic experience, then one fails entirely to grasp the nature of the Holocaust.

Several people who observed the presentation said that the word "attack" was spoken more often than any other word during the discussion. In academic presentations a clear statement of disagreement is often experienced as an "attack" by the followers of an established belief. Many in the audience felt under attack, and Fred of course felt under attack himself. I am writing about a process I have termed "the emotional assimilation of knowledge," and I am seeking to make sense of a presentation where the experience of attack seemed to make knowledge assimilation impossible.

The word "attack" has particular resonance when it is used not to describe a distant event, but to mobilize urgent and powerful defense. There is considerable irony that the claim, "They attacked our ships" is not in its motivational impact a claim about fact. It is an appeal to make an attack on people who have demonstrated themselves to be dangerous.

People in the process of metaphorically "attacking somebody" often imagine themselves defending other people. Perhaps this reflects something about the experience of giving papers. We often have some link to our own emotional state, but we see our opposition as acting only in relation to some principle of reason, that is usually "violated" in some important way in every objection that someone else makes to our own argument.

I believe that the general model of this attack on the ability to think is something we scholars characteristically do, in the assumption that we are doing something useful or "thoughtful." This is all too often the characteristic pattern of academic performance.

It is easy to support the claim that there was nothing dangerous in Professor Alford's ideas. But in this particular situation, the "danger" of Professor Alford's beliefs was not a thought that anyone experienced as needing support. The danger was experienced immediately in the raw emotional intensity of debate. Sentences that would not normally light up with amygdala fight/flight intensity, generated this intensity in the context of that presentation.

Our emphasis on research, reason, and verbal mastery make us unprepared for the events that undermine our own reason. Academics frequently "fight" over verbal claims as if emphatic repetition in vigorous debates could be the occasion for persuasion. Most of us inwardly recognize that when words are experienced as combat, the "force" of thought has no persuasive force whatever. In such cases words are injuries and are experienced directly as such.

I am interested in the Alford presentation because it is representative of a real subject where we are tempted to think that "proper" modes of thought can contain or prevent catastrophic events such as the Holocaust. Encounters like this occur rather frequently at academic presentations. People will leave when they feel the "level" of discourse "degenerates" to the angry repetitions of competing claims. And yet we academics seem unable to formulate, circulate, and recognize a generalized understanding of this failure of thought.

We seem unable to stop ourselves from a practice that seems to insist on the sheer repetition of truth claims. And I should speak personally here. Even though I am making this argument about the failure of thought in the angry repetition of truth claims, I am too often unable myself to recognize and stop this practice. I need other people to point out what I am doing.

Those of us who have dedicated our professional lives to the ethos and practice of the "academic conference" can immediately recognize the mode this particular discussion took. Often you see people leaving a conference room when this intensity of debate emerges. I believe that this practice was and, in most cases, is a ritual of academic behavior that defines as "thought" a practice that is in fact an attack on thought.

The Fred Alford March 2010 presentation is a useful representation of the three problems common in formal academic "thinking": (1) Presentations commonly result in a loss of thought; (2) This loss of thought is supported by a failure of the recognition of the loss of thought; and (3) The loss of thought can be celebrated as a particularly successful practice of thought. (We won.)

In this case I knew most of the people involved. I felt that they had considerable capacity for self-reflection and self-observation. I knew that I wanted to write about this event when I witnessed it. I wrote to many people to ask about what they saw and felt at the time and afterward. I discovered much more than I anticipated in the responses I received.

I wrote to Fred a second time to ask more emphatically about his experience as opposed to his ideas. As I had organized the conference on trauma, my mind was filled with associations that suggested that his experience of talking about trauma had in fact been traumatic.

Fred's first response, as I quoted, was one that reviewed mentally his own argument. He represents his experience as one of the verbal thoughts of the paper. This is how most people "think." They are engaged with their verbal productions. There is another way to think about verbal production, one more reflective of an internal emotional state. The second time I wrote Fred, I asked him for a more "experience near" report. Fred had the training and this skill to observe his thinking and he responded to my email with an interesting confession:

> Marshall, I've been thinking about your desire for an experience near account of my trauma talk, "Was the Holocaust Traumatic?" at Trauma 2010 and the trauma it may have caused me. In fact, I can't stop thinking about it. I can say a couple of things in retrospect. (Fred Alford, email to author, March 12, 2010)

I am taking three points out of six that strike me as particularly useful. Fred reports:

3. Is that experience traumatic? Yes, it is for me. It makes me feel lost and stupid. Your smart blond friend, the thin fellow with black eyeglasses (where is he from?) summarized a version of my argument contra Caruth better than I, which I both admired and was aware I could not, or at least did not, do. He was in touch with the flow of the issues in a way that I had lost it. I had lost the flow.
4. In looking at my notes, I see that where I stopped was immediately after talking about Blanchot's "knowledge as disaster."
5. In group relations conferences in the Tavistock tradition, consultants often talk about being made to feel stupid by the group... I would say that is what I experienced, whether it was imposed by the group or not: that I lost the feel for my own argument. I could say the words, but lost the feel. (Fred Alford, email to author, March 12, 2010)

I was present for the entire event. I saw all the main participants engaged in a heated debate. But I did not see that Fred experienced a sense of self-doubt and loss of thought. He was the eminently capable senior scholar at the presentation. His report of this moment of loss of connection is remarkable. I shall try to argue that this event—what was most invisible in the presentation—was the most important event of the presentation. It was a moment when Fred experienced the loss of safety, the fear that all honest thinkers can encounter if they fully listen to an opposing position.

Fred says that he "lost the feel" of his argument. Writing teachers will sometimes observe that speech derives from some felt sense of experience. This felt sense gives shape and meaning to our utterances. Fred wrote his talk, probably over many hours, securely linked to the "feel" of his argument. At the moment he feels identified with his attackers, however, he loses his connection to his own inner experience. It is as if a chasm has opened up between himself as a speaking being and his audience. If he identifies with them, he loses connection to his own memories. This strikes me as very similar to the experience I described responding to my Marx class in chapter two.

Trauma is, by definition, a condition that generates "dissociation." Dissociation is the psychological "injury" that separates a person from the coherence of their own thought. Fred reports that, in giving a talk on trauma, he experiences a traumatic injury to his own thought. I do not intend this claim as a metaphor, but as a literal description of what happened.

It may seem a stretch to imagine words cause trauma. Trauma is the effect of actions, not words. But in some contexts, words are not words, but actions. We protect people from hate speech, language that provokes attack. We have good reason to do so. We should consider as well that just as words are actions, so also actions are meanings. If a soldier in combat experiences his friends transformed to hamburger by a mortar, he is himself not physically harmed by the event. He is only a witness. And yet this experience can contribute to physical changes in the brain. Meanings have biological effects. When Fred fails to connect his thoughts, we do not see a biological change in the brain but we see the loss of connection in meaning that characterizes traumatic dissociation.

The Emotional Ecology of Educational Space

Liberal arts classrooms provide space for connecting thoughts separated by anxious avoidance. They offer possibilities for reflection. The emotional space of the classroom respects moments when students must face the fear of thought. Academic presentations, in contrast, can create unreasonable fear. They can create gaps between thoughts when such gaps might otherwise not exist. It is as if the drama and war of the presentation calls into play polarizing and paranoid-making thought. Small group bondings in response to shared vulnerabilities quickly create emotional contexts where linkings in thought become undermined.

Academics must take responsibility for contributing to a more complex understanding of the world. And this necessarily means academics have to disagree with established belief systems. And this means writing "provocative" papers. But if established practices for professional development undermine the skills that educators need, we must reevaluate our practices.

In recent years it has become not uncommon for a member of the audience to respond to a talk by saying, "When you say x, it makes me very angry." This kind of admission can be very helpful as it pointedly represents the emotional dynamics of the interaction. Most often when remarks like this are made, they lead simply to the acknowledgment that the speaker has failed to recognize some politically important point of view. Sometimes there is discussion over the importance of this failure and often the speaker simply acknowledges his regret at not having seen the political implications of statement x.

I have never seen the statement, "Statement x makes me very angry," lead to something more exploratory in terms of how one's emotional state supports or hinders reverie or reflective depth. Reflective depth is something we seek as people. It is a skill we must exercise to grow. But it is not something we are encouraged to talk about.

The emotional injuries that we inflict and also experience while giving papers is what we do not talk about. If there is an ethics of academic life, it is that we swallow our injured pride and shame. We are trained to produce words; we focus upon the ideas presented. We put our feelings at the back of our minds and we concentrate on our thinking. We strive for clarity. We act as if arguments can be won by the simple insistent repetition of the "truth." We act as if reason can overcome traumatized minds. When it becomes obvious to others that the increased repetition of an uncomfortable claim only increases an opponent's anger, it is often not obvious to us. We are thinking about other things. A second order act of reflection, one that examines relations between verbal statements and emotion, is not part of our training. Quite the opposite. We are frequently asked to treat the emotional experience of thought with contempt.

This small event is, of course, only one minor battle in the "theory wars." But if it is a "minor battle," it is also a significantly memorable event in a scholar's life. Fred wrote in response to my request for a close account of the experience. "I've been thinking about your desire for an experience near account of my trauma talk, "Was the Holocaust Traumatic?" at Trauma 2010 and the trauma it may have caused me. In fact, I can't stop thinking about it." (Fred Alford, email to author, March 11, 2009). The thinking that Fred talks about is the processing of painful information and the assimilation of this information into a repertoire of knowledge about the world. Fred has managed the pain of his presentation without vilifying the members of his audience. Other scholars are not always so generous. Our capacity for growth depends upon our wisdom in the management of such embattled events.

I wish to thank Fred for his permission to quote from his personal emails.

Chapter Five
Information Relays and the Touched Nerves of Global Injustice

Our species works with a brain best suited to surviving prehistoric threat. We are biologically not well suited for, or perhaps are even maladapted for, surviving the current world problems. We are quick to recognize our primary social group as our place of safety. We risk or sacrifice our individual lives for the sake for the group and we idealize this behavior as one that bestows social prestige and cultural capital. We follow leaders who are quick to identify enemies and aggressive in their determination to destroy threats. We are socialized into discourse systems that energize words with danger when none exists.

We respond quickly to threats to the primary group, but the quickness of our response lacks discriminating attention. We are biologically disabled in our ability to examine and solve problems that require careful discrimination and thorough accumulation and synthesis of information. Responses to attack, such as going to war with Iraq after a terrorist attack, are common amygdala-driven responses to the experience of aggression. In such contexts, calls for thought are more threatening than the real source of danger.

The example of Fred Alford's talk suggests that even when smart and responsible academics devote years of work to understanding the most pressing of human problems—trauma—the very practice of rigorous thinking sets up modes of verbal allegiance that, like group loyalty, make flexible thought difficult. Just as most people develop strong loyalties to family and close friends, so also passionate thinkers develop a loyalty to ideas and systems of thought. Debates that examine ideas can quickly become events that enact the evil both sides strive to avoid. In Alford's presentation both sides to the debate were responsible, thoughtful people seeking to avoid trauma by understanding it. In the process of supporting and sharing their ideas, they destroyed possibilities for synthetic reasoning.

We mobilize for war in response to ideas that pose no threat to us whatsoever, except for the threat of thinking. We then paradoxically fail to respond to developments that careful scientific thinkers argue threaten us with catastrophe. The biological inheritance that makes us quick to respond to threats rooted in an immediate experience of attack, registered with great intensity by the amygdala, makes us slow to respond to threats such as global warming that are recognized only by a very abstract reasoning. In these situations, the divisiveness of political parties makes it all too possible for warnings about threats, from an opposition party, to become threats themselves. Warnings about a problem—and calls for thinking about a problem—become a problem. If the Democrats want climate protection, it is the mobilization of the Democrats, not global warming, that threatens the Republican party. In this manner thinking about a solution to a problem mobilizes opposition to needed information.

Thus far my focus has been upon how particular minds fail or succeed in taking in information. I have sought to offer an initial exploratory description of conditions under which human emotion facilitates or enables the assimilation of information. I argued that conditions of shame, anger, and intimidation are not useful contexts for the assimilation of information and may contribute to dissociation.

In this last chapter I want to expand my perspective to consider information circulation from a global perspective. I will shift my focus from an individual mind in a small face-to-face community to information circulating within a global media. Classroom teachers have some control over the emotional tone of their class and therefore can make use of the emotional contexts that impede or facilitate thought. Online information distribution lacks face-to-face interaction and the emotional dynamics of such learning invites some systematic consideration.

As information distribution becomes increasingly diverse and prolific, we both benefit and suffer. There is more information available and more information available more quickly. But as major news networks compete for viewers, information increasingly becomes sound bites represented out of context and increasingly in contexts that serve to entertain more than to educate. People attend to news prepackaged for particular political agendas. Minds passively receive and contain unassimilated information. Little is done to promote thoughtful integration.

Americans choose their news to match their political bias. Fox News and CNN have significant viewers, but popular news people stage debates that subordinate the possibilities for reflective thought to the need for theatrical rhetorical victories over the opposition.

A central problem that educational systems must address is an improved use of the information we gather. Can we, as educators, foster learning communities better able to make use of vast resources of information? Can global networks of information offer more promise for social progress?

Today information comes in to every computer user from literally every part of the globe. State-controlled media can no longer control the information that massively circulates. Information gathering can be instant; victims of violence can report their stories directly. We need not rely on reporters to interpret events.

This influx of information is available at the same time as college teaching moves into two new practices. First, courses in the humanities increasingly feature themes of social justice. Second, college courses increasingly become online courses that make use of global Internet information. This confluence of increased commitment to social justice with increased information about social injustice leads to interesting questions about the possibilities of using Internet resources and their prolific up-to-the-minute information to solve global problems.

Would it be possible to establish a network of interactions so that information about global problems would be directed to classrooms whose disciplinary purpose would be to solve them? Would it be possible to formulate in a minutely systematic manner a network of global information coordinated with a network of experts committed to understanding and solving global problems? A central requirement for the principle of information relays would be for information to go to people who would have the capacity to assess and respond effectively to the problems presented. It should be relatively easy to systematically establish relays of information that could organize logical patterns of problem solving. Medical needs would go to doctors, legal needs would go to lawyers, agricultural needs would go to agriculturalists. But how do emotional interactions fit in all this? Can we conceptualize a network of emotional relays that might also organize responses to global problems? Are some needs more intense than others, more immediate than others, more demanding than others? Can the emotional assimilation of information be theorized at a global level?

Global Media and the One-Body World of Information Distribution

As I write this manuscript I am attentive to information that Rama Lakshmi reports from the *Washington Post*. In New Delhi:

> Hundreds of Indians poured into the streets of New Delhi on Saturday to mourn the death of a young woman who was gang raped nearly two weeks ago in an incident that triggered a national conversation about violence against women.
> Police announced that the six men arrested in connection with the attack were charged with murder after the woman, who suffered a brain injury and other internal damage, died in a hospital in Singapore, where she had been taken for care. (Lakshmi, 2012)

This story suggests that ad hoc social practices develop spontaneously in response to gross injustice. Many events rise above the usual noise of daily news and "strike us," generating media attention and widespread concern. I am informed by the article that women in India do not feel safe in reporting rape to the police. As I feel concern over this problem, my own concern, amplified by the concern of a million other media readers, contributes to a heightened social awareness that can have an extensive reach and thus change local practices. Rama Lakshmi connects the minds of many people and focuses this mind on a problem that has been ongoing, but not fully confronted. Rama Lakshmi continues:

> Activists say that such cases illustrate why sexual violence largely goes unreported in India. In recent years, New Delhi has earned the title of being the "rape capital" of the nation. This year, more than 560 cases of rapes have been reported. But activists say that only a small fraction of sex crimes are reported in India.
> "The biggest fear that a woman faces when she summons the courage to report rape or sexual harassment is that she will be judged

and labeled as a morally loose woman by the police, by the medical officer, lawyer and judge," said Suman Nalwa, deputy commissioner of police who heads the crime against women cell in New Delhi. (2012)

The story seems to have, as they say, "touched a nerve" regarding the injustice and insensitivity many women feel in India about police response to rape. The story indicates that men can rape women and then—if women complain—they are labeled as morally loose. Injustices such as this are particularly bitter. Women are put in a situation where complaints about injustice become opportunities for more injustice. Women are physically raped and then psychically raped if they complain.

The metaphor of "touching a nerve" here may be more literal than it seems at first glance. Just as nerve cells within a brain connect information about pain in one point of the body to the executive functions of the brain, so also the story of one woman's pain, spreading by "touched nerves" and Internet relays to global points of awareness and so also there developing a widespread social response. And this response has practical effects. Policemen visiting a site of rape in New Delhi will not able to think about this rape with the same mind that they had prior to media coverage. They will be aware that a large public will be giving attention to their actions. This terrible rape story offers some promise that widespread public attention will change current procedures used by the Indian police in their response to rape.

As humans all over the world respond to this story, they organize to produce "executive functions" to monitor better responses to rape in India. I am interested in the logic behind this description of human response to trauma—people "organize" in their response. It is as if some impetus of information coming from the outside world has an effect on the organization of the biological brain. People hear information. They perceive a threat and they "organize" in response. To what extent is this social phenomenon of organization similar to the process whereby the biological brain with a particular individual becomes better "organized" to recognize and respond to danger?

In the human brain better organization allows an executive function to more effectively monitor and respond to problems that need solutions. If we suffer a car accident after heavy snowfall, we are likely to pay more careful attention to these conditions. We are likely to explore what kind of tires, what kind of car, or what kind of snow creates problems. We bring careful attentive conscious thought to bear on activities that hitherto merited little attention.

Human communities organize themselves in relation to problems in a manner roughly analogous to how individual human brains organize in response to problems. There is more acute attention to the indicators of a problem and vigilant attention to the details of the problem.

Reporters in India and elsewhere will seek to respond with more interest to reports of rape and keep an eye on police practices. Social activists with both local and global links will report such information to a larger global community that will, like many women in Delhi, feel outrage at such injustice. Two weeks after the initial report of the rape, Ashok Sharma reported in the *Washington Times* that:

> The attack has led to calls for tougher rape laws and reforms of a police culture that often blames rape victims and refuses to file charges against accused attackers. The nation's top law enforcement official said the country needs to crack down on crimes against women. (2013)

It is as if spontaneous social response often evolves material conditions for the management of social problems. If the police in India have been inattentive to the suffering of raped women, world response brings organized attention to this problem. The very policemen who were inattentive five years ago are likely to be more attentive after the media response. The awareness of media attention increases the attention given to the problem by the policemen.

If these networks of linked individuals caring about the conditions of injustice in the world are now developing spontaneously without plan or system, what would be required to set in place an efficient system to represent instances of social injustice and respond to them effectively?

In *Far from the Madding Crowd* Thomas Hardy presents a character who looks outward to the night sky and imagines that all the external world might be linked up in its organization to one body: "The sky was clear—remarkably clear—and the twinkling of all the stars seemed to be but throbs of one body, timed by a common pulse" (Hardy [1874] 2001, 8). Critics describe Hardy as a novelist very much attentive to the sufferings of the world. He tried to imagine how a more just world might be organized.

Hardy's fantasy of a world experienced as a single body suggests a model for Internet organization. Currently our bodily differences, situated in relation to different social contexts, make us indifferent to the suffering of those different from ourselves.

Can the assimilation of global information function according to a principle similar to the recognition of pain within a single body? That is, can masses of people respond to extreme pain in the body on one particular person with acutely responsive recognition? Can diverse and conflicted groups of people respond to information about suffering as if this particular pain were registered in a shared body? Or, more specifically, can one global "executive function" (mind) tend to the pain manifest in various sites of one world body?

Key to this project is a technique for making the pain of others resonate within ourselves. Hardy imagines a universe where the stars pulse with the rhythm of one body. One repeated claim about art calls attention to its ability to take us into the bodily experience of others. Much has been written about "sympathetic" fiction and narrative empathy. Although scholars debate how effective literature is for organizing social action, some works have clearly contributed significantly to social politics.

Scholars applying the research of cognitive science to film now describe how our mirror neurons may make our recognition of others, made to resonate through the character of art, organically linked to our own inner experience (Elsaesser and Hagener 2010). Through film we can, in some measure, see the faces of others and "feel their pain." "From the point of view of these mirror neurons there appears to be no difference between seeing and doing" (Elsaesser and Hagener 2010, 78). In bringing the faces of distant others before us, film seems to offer unique opportunities for the emotional assimilation of knowledge.

Does artistic form, as a principle of emotional information, offer opportunities for improved global communication? Can Internet communication, linked to artistic forms of information recognition, better foster a one-world Internet body? How might an individual body be a model for a network of information gathering, information assimilation, and active response?

Global Information and Information about Suffering

Can Hardy's one body metaphor inspire an Internet system that would efficiently distribute global information to insure maximum beneficial response to problems? The Internet now brings extensive information about our world to each home. If the rape victim in India "strikes a nerve" in me as an American, can this principle be developed as an educational practice? The task we face is the efficient emotional assimilation of information.

In most colleges and universities the emphasis upon a liberal arts education has given way to an emphasis upon online education. Here at George Washington University faculty have been encouraged to develop virtual versions of their courses. Many professors are seeking formats that can effectively deliver their course material to students who are attending the course in the privacy of their homes. The promises of such courses are staggering. Instead of teaching 20 students, expert teachers can now teach 10,000 students. Through the Internet, human links that were confined to small groups of 20 seem able to expand to link, over time, 100,000 individuals.

My university is considering, in addition, a more ambitious agenda—massive open online courses, or MOOCs. In January 2013 reporter Spencer Michels of PBS delivered a feature story, noting the huge impact of these courses upon global culture. Michels reports that a start-up company, Coursera, currently offers free online courses to 170 thousand students around the world. These classes, he reports, "may be revolutionizing higher education."

Leaders in the online education recognize that "face time" between faculty and students is important to the education process. The concept of face time represents one vestige of the old liberal arts ideal. Education is not just about facts, but about relationships between teachers and students as a vital dynamic in the learning experience. Online educators recognize an element of vitality in this relationship, and seek to find some way in which this body-to-body connection, with its vital emotional resonances, can operate.

Pure online environments would seem to offer few opportunities for face time. But scholars have made useful attempts to find substitutes for this experience. Marisol Clark-Ibanez and Linda Scott propose an online educational model where "student learning comes first and the technology follows" (2008, 34). They argue that "learning happens through interaction and active participation" (Clark-Ibanez and Scott 2008, 34). If interaction becomes human-to-human interaction, there are possibilities for online education to "touch nerves" and integrate global problems with thinkers committed to seeking global solutions.

Although we are a long way from real time real human interaction in online education, very subtle qualities of human "interaction and active participation" can, in theory, be enhanced by online education. I can imagine that emotional cues that often go unnoticed and thus function unconsciously in real classrooms might be given conscious attention through online technologies. Just as film now shows facial close-ups at crucial moments of human interaction, so also online education might make emphatic use of facial expressions in student interactions. These possibilities, as far as I know, remain unexplored. But they are not, in principle, excluded from the thinking of online educators. One principle to explore in Internet education is the extent to which the experience can offer a genuine experience of relating emotionally to other really present people in real time. How much depth can this emotional relationship reach? Can Internet technology use visual media to enhance the emotional connection of student to student and student to teacher?

Currently the professor and other students in an Internet class seem very remote indeed. But can technology amplify rather than reduce this relationship? If technology can allow people to develop very intense relationships to media personalities, can it encourage similar intense relationships with fellow students or professors?

Researchers at MIT Barry Kort, Rob Reilly, and Rosalind W. Picard argue: "Expert teachers are very adept at recognizing and addressing the emotional state of learners and, based upon their observation they take some action that positively impacts learning" (Kort, Reilly, and Picard 2001, 1) Kort, Reilly, and Picard have sought to explore this postulate in some detail through computer-based learning. These researchers first set up an emotional grid to define adaptive and maladaptive emotional learning states. Then, they describe a software that would allow a computer to "observe" a learner's emotional state. If human response is inappropriate to the learning task, the computer responds. Seeking to conceptualize an appropriate software for this interaction, the authors suggest:

> This device will, for example, intervene when a learner is not focused on the relevant part of the computer, or is focused completely outside the task area...Such behavior would trigger an appropriate intervention. (Kort, Reilly, and Picard 2001, 4)

Kort, Reilly, and Picard are correct in observing that "expert teachers are very adept at recognizing and addressing the emotional state of learners." It is reassuring that academics who work with computer-assisted learning recognize the usefulness of emotional responses to learning. What more might computer-driven learning do to increase and facilitate this interaction?

Sharon Joy Ng Hale points out that online education can give shy students a better chance to participate and observe, as well as that "being online gives students the opportunity to reflect on their answers before participating in discussions" (Hale 2007, 31). Clark-Ibanez and Scott quote from a shy student who feels intimidated in a "face to face class." And they quote a student who feels that "discussion" can be more effective in an online class:

> I like [online classes] better because everyone gets to speak and say what they are thinking without the risk of being laughed at. Even the shyest person who might never speak in a regular classroom gets his/her point across in this online discussion. We all get a chance to speak. (Clark-Ibanez and Scott 2008, 35)

It is significant that student evaluations of the online course give particular emphasis to the emotional interactions of learning. Online courses, it seems, give an increased security to some students. Students have more time to think before they "talk." As face-to-face encounters are more distant, students can profit from not being subjected to shame. When online discussions are planned so that everyone gets feedback, students can feel rewarded at being recognized as thinkers in discussions.

This emphasis upon the deeply social nature of classroom experience reminds us once again that thinking is rooted in deeply emotional contexts.

Effective teachers facilitate dialogue and understanding across differences in identity. In real time face time classrooms, experienced teachers can—to some degree—manage the emotional dynamics of classroom interaction. They can encourage classrooms where there is just enough emotional challenge for students to feel curious about otherwise emotionally disruptive information. Effective teachers work to control the emotional climate that facilitates learning. Classrooms must be neither too hot nor too cold. Classroom that are too cold do not allow for emotional expression to emerge. Thinking is shallow and located within emotionally meaningful contexts. Classrooms that are too hot, such as the situation of Fred Alford's talk, foreclose flexible thought by eliminating more complex brain activity.

As all real thinking is grounded in real time, real emotional contexts, these contexts must be thoroughly explored if online teaching is to encourage growing minds to find an effective place in relation to important issues of the day.

In chapter two I described Geoffrey Harpham's talk on the humanities at The University of Damascus in Syria. He describes his perception of his audience as a real time response to ideas: "As I spoke, I imagined that they were not offended. In fact, through the myriad ways a silent audience can communicate with a lecturer, my listeners seemed to me to be particularly focused, almost as if they found the argument interesting" (Harpham 2010, 6). Harpham's mind is alert, not only to his subject, but also to the "myriad ways a silent audience can communicate with a lecturer." This dimension of human interaction is currently not available in online education.

Harpham demonstrates how a good teacher often looks to his students for cues that fine tune emotional connection. When must a teacher slow down a presentation and how must a teacher unpack particular terms? When should a teacher invite a student to articulate a question or an objection? How should a teacher manage the intensity of an emotional interaction? Harpham's narrative indicates that teachers work productively with these principles—but often tacitly and implicitly rather than consciously. Harpham does not explicitly describe how this information is conveyed but he seems to take his cues from reading the emotion on faces, in the immediate relation to the reception of ideational content.

Can online courses be similarly responsive to real time real emotional interaction between professor and student? I feel a strong attachment to my own experience with small interactive face-to-face classes. But it would be foolish to blindly idealize old practices. Perhaps technology could devise procedures to help teachers lacking the skill Harpham exhibits. Certain visual media can bring to our attention the close presence of a distant face. Visual media linked to appropriate software can interrupt a flow of information with visual representations of faces receiving such information. If software can recognize faces, can it also "read" emotion on faces and inform teachers of relations between the informative content of a course and the nature of students' interaction with such content?

The Online Emotional Assimilation of Knowledge

It is not surprising that professors who are called upon to develop online classes show reluctance. Online education is still far more popular among university administrators than among faculty. A 2012 Babson Survey prepared for the journal *Inside Higher Ed* reveals: "Faculty members are far less excited by, and more fearful of, the recent growth of online education than are academic technology administrators."

Faculty "fear" in response to increasing demand for online classes points perhaps to the discomfort most of us feel about teaching an anonymous audience. Even if we do not pay emphatic attention to the faces we teach, they confirm our presence and contribute to our experience that teaching is "real." Emotion marks the lived presence of thought's value in the classroom.

In some ways, classroom teaching has become more emotional. Engaged discussion of political issues is common. Over the last 20 years academics have grown suspicious of neutral political positions. The critiques of Foucault and other postmodern thinkers have made it difficult to for anyone to imagine taking a position that is truly politically neutral.

Politicized teaching often means that educational issues are located in emotional hot spots. It is hard to discuss these without emotional overheating.

As more professors commit to political positions, classroom discussions become "hotter" for students. This can be very useful. But heat itself does not produce flexible minds. Bion argues that under normal conditions our thoughts are mobilized by emotion, not by any logic of thought. We endorse what we love and denounce what we hate and then, to minimal extent, justify our assertions by means of some semblance of reason. Heated political debate, for these reasons, can be a condition for the defeat of thought.

We develop political ideas as we form emotional bonds with people who help us to feel safe and valuable. As this bonded group responds to threats and develops discourse to manage threat, words and concepts become God terms that organize thought and establish safety. When we encounter people with different ideas and other ways of speaking, they can be experienced as threats. Teachers working with political issues have to mediate between discourse groups hostile to each other's respective ideals.

Arousal is a basic principle of mental function. Thought follows a principle of changes in perception, changes in attention, and changes in the intensity of attention. Arousal is not an action we perform by will. Arousal comes to us when "the situation," as they say, "demands attention." Offline resources of the brain are brought "online" by the arousal systems of emotional response. Good teaching works with optimum levels of arousal. Good classes are alert and awake, and enlivened by the play of thought. The management of arousal allows thought to operate above the low levels of boredom and below the high levels of traumatic disorganization.

Traumatic disorganization takes place when the emotional issues of a class cannot be contained by thought. Fred Alford's conference presentation, discussed in chapter four, is a good example of traumatic disorganization. Classrooms can become traumatically disorganized very quickly. Online groups, with their apparently distant links between virtually present participants, can also very quickly "flame" into traumatic disorganization.

Teachers have to be effectual facilitators if they are to make effective use of the emotional heat of political arguments. One potential strategy for managing the emotional heat of political debate would be to focus more efficiently on the experienced emotional justification for political action. All too often, motives for political action derive, not from real experiences of real people who suffer, but from political beliefs about what is good and what is bad for other people. Conservatives, for example, often seek to act politically in order to support free markets, or to put an end to something they consider sinful. Liberals might seek to act in order to support free speech without considering whether such speech contributes to more or greater suffering. Marxists, with their beliefs, might act in a similar way. They may oppose a capitalist business venture without examining to what extent such a venture might or might not have positive effects on real people. In all these cases, one might argue, politics becomes a defensive process whereby one group tries to impose its fantasies upon another group. The very activity of politics, when it is driven by these motives, works not to alleviate human suffering, but to cause it.

A more useful measure of politics might be made in terms of human experiences of suffering. If classes could respond more to the raw data of suffering rather than to the raw emotion of individuals thinking about politics, political agreements might be more common. Political progress in the last two hundred years has been greatly facilitated by bringing communities closer to the concrete experience of injustice. People removed from conditions of slavery might be persuaded that slaves lived happy, contented lives. But firsthand narratives, such as those by Frederick Douglas, made such beliefs tenuous ([1845] 2012).

Two principles might facilitate the emotional assimilation of political information in online classes. First, it is possible to make better use of the immediacy of emotional experience in the digital classroom. Digital media can put in front of us the faces of mothers confronting mass starvation in Mali. Digital media can make us almost present in the real conditions of life very remote from our comfortable American suburbs. This power has the potential to overcome some of the obscuring layers of misrepresentation that attends verbal media representation.

Second, we can work more determinedly to justify politics in terms of immediate emotional experience. The real experiences of real people can be the only legitimate justification for political action. Any alternative justification for politics is bad politics. Information is most important when it is used to solve human problems. This human use of information always has an emotional component because human problems, by definition, involve suffering or the threat of suffering. Most humans suffer when they are in the presence of another who suffers. Political information must draw upon emotional experience and must be considered in an emotional context if it is to be integrated with problem-solving thought.

Internet links offer unique possibilities for delivering information about suffering to large numbers of people. Information about suffering can be represented with more immediacy and nuance. Media participants can document information persuasively and they can reach large numbers of people instantaneously. In this manner the abstractions that have for centuries represented other people in other places can, in part, be overcome. Additionally, we have, in the last 20 years in the humanities, developed an ethos of wanting to know more about others. We seek "to register the experience of the other in progressively more profound and also more useful ways" (Charles 2004, 1).

I propose that we use technology in more creative ways to make the suffering that motivates politics more visible. This technology suggests that if we are all "linked-up" by the world web, we can experience a kind of "one body" connection to human suffering that Hardy imagines in *Far from the Madding Crowd*. There is an implicit political argument in this comparison. Political arguments divide us as groups differently identified with political motivations. We need methods to synthesize divisions that often make political action impossible. More direct and immediate experiences of human suffering may help us overcome divisions. The individual person does not usually experience paralysis in response to experiential calls for action. Individual brains may observe competing claims for action, as when the pain of hunger competes with the hurt of an injured finger. The body with its 100 billion neurons in the brain and 60 trillion synapses in the cerebral cortex alone integrates information from the internal body and the external world in order to make response to suffering quick and efficient. The demands of the stomach, in its need for food, are compared with the demands of the finger, in its need for attention, and the mind acts on an unconscious but effectively assimilated "understanding" of the greater need.

The gang rape of an unnamed paramedical student in India represents positive possibilities for global politics. It is as if the global body acts like the individual biological body. We are "struck" by a recognition of suffering and instinctive demand for action. Linked expressions of concern bring enormous pressure to bear upon local officials who can no longer think about moral issues the same way.

But there limitations in the ability of the Internet to unify bodies already pre-organized by historically specific memories of injustice. But if the rape injustice in New Delhi represents the positive potential for global information, the 9/11 twin tower attacks betray the weak spots in global information relays.

The pain of the 9/11 attacks was transferred differently to different national "bodies." This awareness of pain, however, did not contribute to an effective global solution to the problem presented by the event. Americans who registered the pain of the event were diminished in their capacity to respond. Established political identities quickly assimilated the information to reinforce established stereotypes of danger and safety.

Law-abiding Muslims throughout America, and, paradoxically, Sikhs who had fought bloody confrontations with Muslims during the partition of India, were all victims of undiscriminating American aggression against a threat that even an American president understood in religious, not political, terminology.

Global Media and Traumatic Disorganization

After 9/11 America gathered around the cause of national defense in a style that exacerbated gaps in thought. Before we could think through real national threats to security, we went to war with a foreign power that did not threaten us. This war cost enormous expenditures of money and thus reduced our capacity to respond to real threats. The war cost many lives, killed many people who did not need to be killed, increased the suspicion of the Muslim world, and did little to reduce the terrorist threat we faced.

This American response to attack, evidence indicates, is not unique. Diplomat and psychiatrist Vamik Volkan argues that large groups frequently organize themselves irrationally around generational memories of a "chosen trauma" (1977, 36–49). In situations of threat, old memories of injury, even old ethnic memories of injury become organizing centers for the synthesis of information. Such an organizing logic is highly unhelpful. Real-world situations are intelligible only in terms of outdated situational categories.

Volkan defines "chosen trauma" as a particular way large groups remember an injury done to them and then use that injury to organize social action and make sense of external threat. Chosen traumas are practices whereby a "large group" unconsciously defines its "identity through the transgenerational transmission of injured selves with the memory of the ancestor's trauma" (Volkan 1977, 36–49). Volkan offers many examples of this. There are Czechs remembering the 1620 battle of Bila Hora, Scots remembering the 1746 battle of Culloden, the Lakota people remembering the massacre at Wounded Knee, the Jews remembering the Holocaust. Volkan describes in rich detail Slobodan Milosevic's six hundredth anniversary celebration of the Battle of Kosovo as a ritual of national unification.

In describing "chosen trauma" as the "mental representation" of a "historical event," Volkan explains how a particular violent historical event defines discourse and organizes individual minds for action. Particular memories of suffering anchor a discourse and appeal passionately to a community's sense of meaning, honor, and safety. Communities seek to avoid shame and take actions that give pride.

If the rape of the paramedical student in India contributed to an "executive function" that gave a hope of greater justice for women in India, the 9/11 attack gave rise to an executive function that gave less hope for justice for non-white Americans and more possibility for violent interaction. It is as if a particular threat could only be imagined as a racial threat or a religious threat, for those modes of representation have served as representations of anxiety in the psyche of white Americans for centuries.

Traumatic events are manipulated with sobering effectiveness by charismatic leaders. Volkan observes: "The political leader of a nation or other group may be seen as the focal point at which the impact of relationships with enemies and with allies is felt and from which such relations are directed toward both" (1988, 5). Social organization motivated by the experience of threat responds pathologically to impassioned leadership. Complex perceptions are reduced as urgent fear reductively organizes contradictory information.

Traumatic Disorganization and the Individual Mind

Chosen trauma, group hysteria, and paranoid delusion mark the failure of large group response to crisis. Such behavior calls into question the hope of a one-body politics. Even if a group could respond to suffering with the organization of one mind, such a mind itself has poor response to trauma. Even if the Internet could link all people together as "one mind," that one mind would still be subject to the internal disorganization of traumatic experience.

Chosen traumas have discursive power precisely to create gaps in memory and gaps in brain functions. Trauma organizes by excluding information. H. D. S. Greenway, in an October 20, 2009, *New York Times* op-ed article, points out that Volkan's chosen trauma describes "the way nations, as well as individuals, can seize upon a wrong done to them to the exclusion of any wrongs committed by themselves."

For Americans, the 9/11 disaster organized discourse as a paranoid logic. It gave Americans an opportunity to increase national solidarity in relation to a chosen trauma defined initially along believer infidel divisions. It is as if the increased intensity of pain associated with national identity contributed to a more intense sense of national identity—and also an increased experience of threat from other people. Mark Bracher, in *Social Symptoms of Identity Needs*, details how President's Bush's war on terror had the character of paranoid thought (2009, 148). There was a great deal of thinking after 9/11. But much of this thinking was paranoid thinking. If I type in the words "paranoid thinking after 9/11" on Google today, January 9, 2013, I immediately get ten sites that offer discussions of this theme of paranoid thought in venues as diverse as *Psychology Today*, CNN, and the British *Guardian*. After over ten years it has become easy to see the problems in American thinking just after the twin towers attack. At the time, however, most of us (I include myself in this group) were unable to think so clearly.

I began this chapter with the intent to explore how human communities might pursue progress toward world justice by using the organizational metaphor of "one body" as a way to link human communication in such a way as to allow information about suffering to travel from one part of the world's body to an executive center, like the brain of a particular body, so that the whole body might be better coordinated in response to suffering. We see this response already in operation. When I and millions of other people respond to the rape in India, I become part of a discourse community outraged at intolerable behavior. The passion of my mind has effects on the mind of a policeman in New Delhi.

But Volkan's analysis of the organization of human communities around chosen traumas suggests that we will have to think carefully about how to use suffering as an anchor for social organization.

The facts of the 9/11 tragedy and our current understanding of trauma challenge the hope of an effective one-world body. Even if the world could be organized in terms of a network of relays organized as "one body," this organization would not guarantee an effective response to global suffering. It is as if the same processes that organize individual minds in response to trauma also organize a social mind in response to trauma. Trauma is the unthinkable. Trauma drives us to the safety of constricted but established patterns of thought. We respond to threats in terms that endanger our capacity for problem solving.

To grasp the nature of a "one mind" Internet connection, we must understand the biology of the mind responding to threat. Internet links are computer links. Minds responding to computer information have a complex biological organization. Emotional stress affects human memory in biological brains much differently than computer memory.

Trauma and stress have biological impacts on biological minds. Trauma and stress contribute to dissociative patterns of thought that undermine a cohesive understanding of problems. Bruce Perry points out: "Traumatic events impact the multiple areas of the brain that respond to the threat. Use-dependent changes in these areas create altered neural systems that influence future functioning" (Perry 2000). Trauma is particularly common and creates a variety of predictable problems with information assimilation. Trauma, like stroke, impairs information flow between the right brain and the left brain.

Current research in neurobiology suggests that trauma reflects disturbances in particular interlinked neural structures. Sarah N. Garfinkel and Israel Liberzon review recent findings from neuroimaging and describe biological changes in PTSD traumatized individuals:

> The findings repeatedly converge on a number of key structures such as the amygdala, ACC, mPFC, insula, and hippocampus. Taken together, the findings lend tentative support to a neurocircuitry model that emphasizes the role of dysregulation in threat-related processing in PTSD. According to this model, trauma exposure sets off a cascade of neural changes that culminates in a

state of amygdala hyperresponsivity to trauma reminiscent and other threat-related stimuli that mediates symptoms of hyperarousal and vigilance associated with PTSD. The model also proposes associated inadequate top-down control by the mPFC and ACC that maintains and perpetuates the state of amygdala hyperresponsivity, and also helps mediate the failure to suppress attention to trauma-related stimuli. (2009, 380)

Interactions among key neural structures, the amygdala, the ACC (anterior cingulated cortex), the mPFC (medial prefrontal cortex), the insula, and the hippocampus are damaged by traumatic experience. It is not simply that brains are damaged by trauma, but that "exposure" to trauma "sets off a cascade of neural changes." Brain performance is damaged by experiences that do not physically harm the body but do very much harm the brain and the mind.

The term "exposure to trauma" means, in effect, an experience of feeling profoundly unsafe in a dangerous world. We can imagine this exposure in very dramatic terms—a combat veteran who was himself wounded when he saw his best friend shredded into multiple body parts by mortar fire. In many cases exposure to trauma can be a much less dramatic, but nonetheless consequential event. Bessell van der Kolk, a leading researcher, describes how long-term neglect in childhood contributes to trauma.

> The traumatic stress field has adopted the term "complex trauma" to describe the experience of multiple, chronic and prolonged, developmentally adverse traumatic events, most often of an interpersonal nature (eg, sexual or physical abuse, war, community violence) and early-life onset. These exposures often occur within the child's caregiving system and include physical, emotional, and educational neglect and child maltreatment beginning in early childhood. (2005, 403)

Van der Kolk argues that "physical, emotional and educational" neglect can contribute to serious deficits in cognition. Trauma in this case is triggered not only by violence inflicted upon a child, but also by failures of response to a child's experience of the world. Trauma is not something that happens; it is the effects of caretaking responses that do not happen. The "caregiving system" must take physical, emotional, and educational care of a child to allow that emerging mind to know itself and be effectively organized in relation to danger.

Van der Kolk collects research to argue that developmental trauma in children is a widespread social problem:

> Chronic trauma interferes with neurobiological development... and the capacity to integrate sensory, emotional and cognitive information into a cohesive whole. Developmental trauma sets the stage for unfocused responses to subsequent stress, leading to dramatic increases in the use of medical, correctional, social and mental health services. People with childhood histories of trauma, abuse and neglect make up almost the entire criminal justice population in the US. Physical abuse and neglect are associated with very high rates of arrest for violent offenses. In one prospective study of victims of abuse and neglect, almost half were arrested for nontraffic-related offenses by age 32. (2005, 403)

Trauma weakens the brain's ability to formulate "cohesive" understanding. In conditions of trauma people often are unable to register and respond to their own suffering. Their response to suffering can be much like the response of Ramachandran's patients with anosognosia. They hallucinate strengths they do not have and they have trouble seeing the world as is.

Van der Kolk's description of trauma suggests that the condition may be more common than we imagine. It is not a condition confined only to those who have suffered memorable violence. It can be a condition of neglect. If so, then this condition of being unable to take in information may be both common and biologically resistant to thought.

I began this book with a story from Ramachandran of a brain unable to take in information regarding its own paralysis. The problem, it seems, is that the left brain cannot effectively communicate with the right brain. We can describe this as a dissociative condition that seriously impairs a person's ability to interact with the world. I end this book with van der Kolk's suggestion that perhaps a quarter of us have traumatically impaired brains. We fail to respond intelligently to information we receive. It is unsettling to consider, as Ramachandran proposes, that people can seem quite sane in every respect, but in relation to one framework for information integration, act essentially psychotic in their inability to see what is literally in front of their nose.

The problem in recognizing suffering has two components. One component is our recognition of the suffering of others. The second is the recognition of our own suffering. Ramachandran's patients with paralyzed arms are unable to recognize that their arms are paralyzed. Trauma represents a core condition that defeats attempts to pursue rational global politics because trauma represents a condition where a traumatized individual is unable to act rationally in relation to their own safety. The person suffering from trauma may do exactly the wrong thing in response to danger. The combat vet wanders into the line of fire, the abused woman takes up a relationship with an abusive man.

Van der Kolk argues that while secure children learn to describe their internal states and know their needs, children with trauma do not:

> Secure children learn a complex vocabulary to describe their emotions, such as love, hate, pleasure, disgust, and anger. This allows them to communicate how they feel and to formulate efficient response strategies. They spend more time describing physiological states such as hunger and thirst, as well as emotional states, than do maltreated children. (2005, 403)

The ability to describe the conditions of one's inner life and the conditions of one's suffering is damaged by "developmental trauma." This damage has many repercussions. If people are unable to recognize our own suffering they will still register this suffering as stress, but be unable to act intelligently to reduce the stress.

Freud developed his understanding of trauma in World War I after working with the condition of "shell shock" where soldiers subject to intense barrages of cannon would "lose their minds" and wander helpless amid the dangers of no-man's-land. Their minds could no longer respond to perceptions of danger. Their actions endangered their own bodies. They were no longer useful as soldiers. Abram Kardiner, an American psychiatrist, defined trauma as "disorganized" experience that affected "executive functions."

When Freud developed his theory of psychoanalysis he gave great emphasis to a mind in conflict with itself, and he used the term "repression" to make sense of how a mind will censor information that generates conflict. Psychiatry departments today, most often, describe the effects of trauma in terms of "dissociation" rather than "repression." Dissociation is not the effect of a mind in conflict with itself, but a mind that has been injured by a harmful event and biologically damaged in terms of its integrative functions. Such a mind, as Bruce Perry points out, cannot integrate the information that is stored in its various memory locations.

Trauma seems to be a constant condition for human communities, and concomitantly, dissociation seems to be a constant feature of human mental life.

In dissociation the human brain cannot fully register nor "add up" the facts that describe human suffering. Dissociation, by definition, is a tendency of the brain to not make problem solving links in thought. Because of trauma, we desire not to know. Rather than linking thoughts in a manner that develops understanding of danger, dissociation fails to make effective use of information already in memory.

Doris Brothers has suggested that we think of trauma as structuring "experiential black holes" in the capacity to think (2008, 51). Her work with trauma patients has led her to see traumatized styles of thought as resistant to the integration of new information:

> While the relational patterns that form within nontraumatized system tend to be orderly and stable, they nevertheless change flexibly with the shifting needs of their constituents. In the language of systems theorists, they are context sensitive. The relational patterns that characterize traumatized system are strikingly different. Emerging within systems dominated by the desperate need to halt the spread of chaos and tormenting uncertainty, they tend to be rigid, restrictive, and impervious to the changing environment. (Brothers 2008, 53)

Albert Einstein is reputed to have said that insanity is doing the same thing over and over again and expecting different results. Unfortunately, the tending to "do the same thing over and over again" is precisely one of the effects of trauma and the failure of information integration. Traumatic repetition was what Freud observed after World War I and has been confirmed by many researchers over the last one hundred years. People will repeat their traumas not only in their dreams but often also in their actual behaviour. This repetition takes place even though it is inappropriate or counterproductive.

Van der Kolk points that the repetition of past events can be triggered when a person misreads a current situation because of traumatic memory. Misreading the present, the traumatized mind repeats a past response and, in the current situation, this dumb repetition causes significant risk or harm:

> Some traumatized people remain preoccupied with the trauma at the expense of other life experiences and continue to re-create it in some form for themselves or for others. War veterans may enlist as mercenaries, victims of incest may become prostitutes, and victims of childhood physical abuse seemingly provoke subsequent abuse in foster families or become self-mutilators. Still others identify with the aggressor and do to others what was done to them. Clinically, these people are observed to have a vague sense of apprehension, emptiness, boredom, and anxiety when not involved in activities reminiscent of the trauma. There is no evidence to support Freud's idea that repetition eventually leads to mastery and resolution. In fact, reliving the trauma repeatedly in psychotherapy may serve to re-enforce the preoccupation and fixation. (van der Kolk 1989, 401)

It is ironic that trauma is the biological response to overwhelming danger and it is also a condition that makes us least thoughtful and masterful in relation to the things that endanger us. Perhaps our primitive ancestors needed to make use of urgent brain impulse to take quick decisions to avoid danger. Most of us no longer need protection from lions or other savanna predators. Instead we need protection from political leaders who have traumatic styles of response to threat. Actions taken by these leaders can have long-term, costly effects. We need to use our frontal lobes to avoid danger. More important we need to develop social practices that teach us to use frontal lobes to avoid danger.

The evidence of trauma suggests that even if global information networks bring essential information to every computer user, there still remains the problem of bringing the information that has reached the computer user into relation with the prefrontal lobes that can do thinking with the information. Hardy's brave metaphor for a more just world offers promise for linking humans together in a responsible and responsive attention to world pain. But this model has limitations. Even if the world were linked together along the model of a single body, the mind of that body might be expected to be unable to respond effectively to traumatic conditions of suffering.

The problem of trauma brings us back, once again, to the crisis of knowing.

Democratic nations recognize the importance of free access to information, rational debate, an open press, and required public education. Schools are valued as important in contributing to the formation of an informed and capable electorate. Universities study the world of human life, produce knowledge, and distribute it in countless forms. But universities do very little to help students assimilate knowledge. If knowledge is produced but not intelligently assimilated, it serves no useful purpose.

Human communities are characteristically organized around threats to that community. To the extent that threat is intensely dramatic, it is also traumatic. The organization of community around a traumatic threat also organizes a mind reluctant to take in information threatening to the community organization. New information that threatens the organization of the community is dissociated; it is not integrated within an executive function. Intensely heated arguments between differently traumatized discourse communities become forms of psychic violence that substitute for physical violence. They offer possibilities for increased traumatization, but they offer little possibility for thought.

A community discourse can be organized as a symptom that protects the mind of the community from the disruption of its own organization. This means that it can only be unconscious of any information that significantly disrupts its organization. Members of a belief system who listen to the speech of an opposing belief system experience dissociation in the ability to think. There is a gap in their ability to take in information. The moment of dissociation is generally unconscious, because the moment-to-moment linking of thought covers the gap in linking by an insistent attachment to other more happy links in representation.

To be organized within a particular passionate discourse community is be organized around the structure of a symptom. This is a condition of thinking for the true believers of many belief systems, be they religious, political, or academic. We become attached to people and ideas we are comfortable with. We become blind to modes of discourse organized around other logics determined by other people with other passions. Symptoms, whether personal or social, are examples of failed discourse organization. But we all, as Zizek says, love our symptoms (Zizek, 1992).

The development of flexible minds and the healing of traumatic disruptions must be a goal pursued determinedly by American colleges and universities. Liberal arts education has long been seen as a producer of more flexible minds. Science now helps us to understand the conditions that encourage this growth. There is much more to learn about how emotional life is interrelated with rational life. It would seem only reasonable that while liberal arts education is costly, its development and refinement are well worth the price. If I say, however, that "it is only reasonable," I discover my argument to be caught within the very powers I have sought to combat. I, and others sympathetic to my analysis, think it is "reasonable" to invest in liberal arts education. But I address an academic community whose passions about education are organized in very diverse and combative styles.

Bibliography

Achebe, Chinua. (1977) 2001. "An Image of Africa: Racism in Conrad's Heart of Darkness." In *The Norton Anthology of Theory and Criticism*, edited by Vincent B. Leitch, William E. Cain, Laurie A. Finke, Barbara E. Johnson, John McGowan, T. Denean Sharpley-Whiting, and Jeffrey J. Williams. New York: Norton.

Alcorn, Marshall. 2001. "Ideological Death and Grief." *JPCS: Journal for the Psychoanalysis of Culture and Society* 6 no. 2 (2001): 172–180.

Aristotle. *Rhetoric*. 2004. Translated by W. Rhys Roberts. Penn State Electronic Classics. http://www2.hn.psu.edu/faculty/jmanis/aristotle/Aristotle-Rhetoric.pdf (accessed Jan. 20, 2013).

Association of American Colleges and Universities. "Statement on Liberal Learning." http://www.aacu.org/About/statements/liberal_learning.cfm (accessed July 20, 2012).

Bain, Ken. 2004. *What the Best College Teachers Do*. Cambridge: Harvard University Press.

Berman, Jeffrey. 1994. *Diaries to an English Professor: Pain and Growth in the Classroom*. Amherst: University of Massachusetts Press.

Bion, W. R. 1959. "Attacks on Linking." *International Journal of Psycho-Analysis* 40. Reprinted in 1967 in *Second Thoughts: Selected Papers on Psychoanalysis*. London: Karnac Books.

———. (1962a) 1977. *Learning from Experience*. London: Seven Servants.

———. (1962b) 1984. "A Theory of Thinking." *Second Thoughts: Selected Papers on Psychoanalysis*, 306–310. London: Karnac Books.

———. 1963. *Elements of Psychoanalysis*. London. William Heinemann.

———. 1965. *Transformations*. London. William Heinemann.

Bisiach, E., M. L. Rusconi, and G. Vallar. 1991. "Remission of Somatophrenic Delusion through Vestibular Stimulation." *Neuropsychologia* 29 (10): 1029–1031.

Bracher, Mark. 2006. *Radical Pedagogy: Identity, Generativity, and Social Transformation*. New York: Palgrave Macmillan.

———. 2009. *Social Symptoms of Identity Needs*. London: Karnac Books.

Brooks, David. 2011. *The Social Animal: The Hidden Sources of Love, Characters, and Achievement*. New York: Random House.

Brothers, Doris. 2008. *Toward a Psychology of Uncertainty: Trauma-Centered Psychoanalysis*. New York: Analytic Press.
Bryson, Bill. 1998. *A Walk in the Woods: Rediscovering America on the Appalachian Trail*. New York: Harper Books.
Burgess, H. 2009. "Working with Strong Emotions in the Classroom: A Guide for Students and Teachers." www.beyondintractability.org/user_guides/teaching_with_emotions/?nid=6578 (accessed June 25, 2009).
Burke, Kenneth. 1950. *A Rhetoric of Motives*, 298–301. Berkeley: University of California Press. Cacioppo, John T., Gary G. Berntson, Shelley E. Taylor, and Daniel L. Schacter, eds. 2002. *Foundations in Social Neuroscience*. Cambridge: Massachusetts Institute of Technology.
Cartwright, R. D. 2004. "The Role of Sleep in Changing Our Minds: A Psychologist's Discussion of Papers on Memory Reactivation and Consolidation in Sleep." *Learning and Memory* 11(6): 660–663.
Caruth, Cathy. 1996. *Unclaimed Experience: Trauma, Narrative and History*. Baltimore: Johns Hopkins University Press.
Charles, Marilyn. 2004. *Learning from Experience: A Guidebook for Clinicians*. New York: Routledge.
Clark-Ibanez, Marisol, and Linda Scott. 2008. "Learning to Teach Online." *Teaching Sociology* 36: 34–41.
Conflicted Faculty and Online Education, *Inside Higher Education*. http://www.insidehigered.com/news/survey/conflicted-faculty-and-online-education-2012.
Conrad, Joseph. (1891) 1988. "An Informal Preface." In *Heart of Darkness*, edited by Robert Kimbrough. Norton Critical Edition. New York: W. W. Norton.
———. (1899) 1988. *Heart of Darkness*, edited by Robert Kimbrough. Norton Critical Edition. New York: W. W. Norton.
Cozolino, Louis. 2002. *The Neuroscience of Psychotherapy*. New York: W. W. Norton.
Cronon, William. 1998. "Only Connect…: The Goals of a Liberal Education." *The American Scholar* 67 (4)(Autumn): 73–80.
Curtis, V., and Adam Biran. 2001. "Dirt, Disgust and Disease: Is Hygiene in Our Genes?" *Perspectives in Biology and Medicine* 44 (1): 17–31.
Damasio, Antonio. 1995. *Descartes Error: Emotion, Reason, and the Human Brain*. New York: Harper Collins.
———. 1999. *The Feeling of What Happens: Body and Emotion in the Making of Consciousness*. Boston: Houghton Mifflin Harcourt.
———. 2003. *Looking for Spinoza: Joy, Sorrow, and the Feeling Brain*. New York: Harcourt Press.
———. 2012. *Self Comes to Mind: Constructing the Conscious Brain*. New York: Random House Books.
Dewey, John. (1916) 2008. *Democracy and Education*. Radford, VA: Wilder Publications.

Dodge, Kenneth. 1991. "Emotion and Social Information Processing." In *The Development of Emotional Regulation and Dysregulation*, edited by Judy Garber and Kenneth Dodge. Cambridge: Cambridge University Press.
Douglas, Frederick. (1845) 2012. *Narrative of the Life of Frederick Douglas, an American Slave*. New York: Gale, Sabin Americana.
Eagleton, Terry. 2007. *Ideology: An Introduction*. 2nd ed. New York: Verso.
Ekman, Paul, E. R. Sorenson, and Friesen Wallace. 1969. "A Pan-Cultural Facial Expression of Emotion." *Science* 164 (3875) (April 4, 1969): 86–88.
Elsaesser, Thomas, and Malte Hagener. 2010. *Film Theory: An Introduction through the Senses*. New York: Routledge.
Farrell, J. G. 1973. *Singapore Grip*. New York: NYRB Classics.
Felman, Shoshona. 1989. *Jacques Lacan and the Adventure of Insight*. Cambridge, MA: Harvard University Press.
Filene, Peter. 2005. *The Joy of Teaching*. Chapel Hill: University of North Carolina Press.
Fish, Stanley. 1999. *The Trouble with Principle*. Cambridge: Harvard University Press.
———. 2001. "Holocaust Denial and Academic Freedom." *Valparaiso University Law Review* 35: 499–526.
Foulkes, David. 1999. *Children's Dreaming and the Development of Consciousness*. Cambridge, MA: Harvard University Press.
Frank, Arthur. 2007. "Five Dramas of Illness." *Perspectives in Biology and Medicine* 50 (3) (Summer): 379–394.
Freud, Sigmund. 1905. "Three Essays on Sexuality." In *The Standard Edition of the Complete Psychological Works of Sigmund Freud*. 24 vols. Edited and translated by James Strachey. London: Hogarth Press, 1953–74, Vol 7, 123–246.
———. 1913. "Totem and Taboo." In *The Standard Edition*, Vol. 13, 1–255.
———. 1915. "Instincts and Their Vicissitudes." In *The Standard Edition*, Vol. 7, 104–140.
———. 1917. "Mourning and Melancholia." In *The Standard Edition*, Vol. 14, 237–260.
———. 1921. "Group Psychology and the Analysis of the Ego." In *The Standard Edition*, Vol. 18, 98–136.
———. 1926. "Inhibitions, Symptoms and Anxiety." In *The Standard Edition*, Vol. 20, 77–179.
Gage, Amity. 2013. *Schroder: A Novel*. New York: Hachett Book Group.
Garfinkel, Sarah N., and Israel Liberzon. 2009. "Neurobiology of PTSD: A Review of Neuroimaging Findings." *Psychiatric Annals* 39: 370–381.
Giroux, Henry A. 2001. *Theory and Resistance in Education: Towards a Pedagogy for the Opposition*, Rev. ed. Westport, CT: Bergin and Garvey.
Goleman, Daniel. 1985. *Vital Lies, Simple Truths: The Psychology of Self-Deception*. New York: Simon & Schuster.

Greenway, H. D. S. 2009. "Cyprus and 'Chosen Trauma.'" *New York Times*, October 20. Op-Ed Contributor. http://www.nytimes.com/2009/10/21/opinion/21iht-edgreenway.html.

Hale, Sharon Joy Ng. 2007. "Being Online." *Academe* 93 (6): 28–32.

Halloun, Inbrahim About, and David Hestenes. 1985. "Common Sense Concepts about Motion." *American Journal of Physics* 53, no. 11 (November): 1056–1065.

Hardy, Thomas. (1874) 2001. *Far from the Madding Crowd*. New York: Modern Library.

Harpham, Geoffrey. 2010. *The Humanities and the Dream of America*. Chicago: University of Chicago Press.

Herman, Judith. 1992. *Trauma and Recovery: From Domestic Abuse to Political Terror*. New York: Basic Books.

Holodynski, Manfred, and Stefanie Kronast. 2009. "Shame and Pride: Invisible Emotions in Classroom Research." In *Emotions as Bio-Cultural Processes*, edited by Hans Markowitsch and Birgit Rottger-Rossler, 371–394. New York: Springer Verlag Press.

Inside Higher Ed. 2013. Growth for Online Learning. Babson Group Survey 2012. http://www.insidehighered.com/news/survey/conflicted-faculty-and-online-education-2012#ixzz2GMSeTe7q.

Jacobs, Dale, and Laura Micciche. 2003. *A Way to Move: Rhetorics of Emotion and Composition Studies*. Portsmouth, NH: Boynon/Cook Publishers.

Kafka, Alexander. 2012. "Eric Kandel's Visions." *The Chronicle of Higher Education*, March 11. http://chronicle.com/article/Eric-Kandels-Visions/131095/.

Kelly, Vernon. "A Primer of Affect Psychology." The Tomkins Institute. www.tomkins.org/Affect_Script_Psyc.html.

Keohane, Joe. 2010. "How Facts Backfire." *Boston Globe*, July 11. http://www.boston.com/bostonglobe/ideas/articles/2010/07/11/how_facts_backfire/ July 11 2010.

Klein, Melanie. 1932. *The Psycho-analysis of Children*. London: Hogarth Press.

Kline, Peter, and Bernard Saunders. 2010. *Ten Steps to Learning Organization*. Salt Lake City: Great River Books.

Kort, B., R. Reilly, and R. W. Picard. 2001. "An Affective Model of Interplay between Emotions and Learning: Reengineering Educational Pedagogy-Building a Learning Companion." In *Proceedings of International Conference on Advanced Learning Technologies* (ICALT 2001), August. Madison, WI. affect.medi.met.edu/publications.php 2001.

Kuklinski, James, Paul J. Quirk, Jennifer Jerit, David Schwieder, and Robert Rich. 2000. "Misinformation and the Currency of Democratic Citizenship." *The Journal of Politics* 62 (3) (August): 790–816.

Lacan, J. 1992. *The Seminar of Jacques Lacan, Book VII: The Ethics of Psychoanalysis, 1959–1960*. Edited by J.-A. Miller and translated by D. Porter. New York and London: Norton.

Lakshmi, Rama. 2012. "National Uproar over Young Woman's Death Triggers Public Conversation about Rape." *Washington Post*, Dec. 29. http://washingtonpost.com/world.

LeDoux, Joseph. 1998. *The Emotional Brain: The Mysterious Underpinnings of Emotional Life*. New York: Simon and Schuster Paperbacks.

Lenzi, J., 2006. "Cyberspace, Identity, and the Passion for Ignorance." In *Pedagogical Desire: Authority, Education, Transference, and the Question of Ethics*, edited by J. Jagodzinski, 169–178. Santa Barbara, CA: Greenwood Press.

Liberty Zone Café. 2006. "Are Americans Practicing Communism?" http://www.libertyzone.com/Communist-Manifesto-Planks.html, Nov. 6 (accessed July 10, 2012).

Mailer, Norman. 1960. *The Naked and the Dead*. New York: Signet Books.

Martin, Daniel, John Garske, and Katherine Davis. 2000. "Relation of the Therapeutic Alliance with Outcome and Other Variables: A Meta-Analytic Review." *Journal of Consulting and Clinical Psychology* 68: 438–450.

Marx, Karl, and Frederick Engels. (1848) 2002. *The Communist Manifesto*. New ed. New York: Penguin Classics.

Masse, Michelle. 2011. "Pointing at the Moon: Teaching and Learning without Resistance." *Educação Temática Digital* 13: 238–245.

Matthiessen, P. 2008. *Shadow Country*. New York. Modern Library.

Meltzer, Donald, and Meg Harris Williams. *The Apprehension of Beauty: The Role of Aesthetic Conflict in Development, Violence and Art*. Old Ballechin, Scotland: Clunie Press, 1988.

Michels, Spencer. 2013. "How Free Online Courses Are Changing the Traditional Liberal Arts Education." *PBS*, Jan. 8. http://www.pbs.org/newhour/bb/education.

Nussbaum, Martha. 2010. *Not for Profit: Why Democracy Needs the Humanities*. Princeton: Princeton University Press.

Nyhan, Brendan, and Jason Reifler. 2010. "When Corrections Fail: The Persistence of Political Misperceptions." *Political Behavior* 32 (2) (March): 303–330.

Olson, Gary, and Lynn Worsham. 2004. "Rhetoric, Emotion, and the Justification of Belief." In *Postmodern Sophistry: Stanley Fish and the Critical Enterprise*, edited by Gary Olson and Lynn Worsham. Albany: SUNY Press.

Patterson, Stephen. 2011. "Does Teaching Critical Thinking Include Challenging Students Beliefs?" *RAIL: A Blog about Reasoning, Argumentation, and Informal Logic*. Dec. 23. http://railct.com/2011/12

/23/does-teaching-critical-thinking-include-challenging-students-beliefs/ (accessed July 23, 2012).
Payne, Jessica D., and Lynn Nadel. 2004. "Sleep, Dreams, and Memory Consolidation: The Role of the Stress Hormone Cortisol." *Learning and Memory* 11(6): 671–678.
Perkins, Charlotte Gilman. (1892) 2002. *The Yellow Wallpaper*. New York: BookSurge Press.
Perry, B. D. 2000. "Traumatized Children: How Childhood Trauma Influences Brain Development." *The Journal of the California Alliance for the Mentally Ill* 11: 48–51. http://www.aaets.org/article196.htm.
Polyp. 2011. "Challenging the Politics of Paranoia." *New Internationalist Magazine* 440 (March). http://newint.org/features/2011/03/01/polyp-conspiracy-theories/ (accessed Aug. 2, 2012).
Porter, Katherine Anne. (1936) 1962. *Pale Horse, Pale Rider*. Signet Books New American Library.
Ramachandran, V. S. 1999. *Phantoms in the Brain: Probing the Mysteries of the Human Mind*. New York: Harper Books.
———. 2012. *The Tell-Tale Brain: A Neuroscientist's Quest for What Makes Us Human*. New York: W. W. Norton.
Ray, Oakley. 2004. "How the Mind Hurts and Heals the Body." *American Psychologist* 59 (1): 29–40.
Revonsuo, Antti. 2000. "The Reinterpretation of Dreams: An Evolutionary Hypothesis of the Function of Dreaming." *Behaviorial and Brain Sciences* 23: 793–1121.
Rokeach, Milton. 1964. *The Three Christs of Ypsilanti*. New York: New York Review Books.
Russell, Bertrand. 1938. Power: A New Social Analysis. London: George Allen and Unwin Ltd.
Samuels, Robert. 2007. *Teaching the Rhetoric of Resistance: The Popular Holocaust and Social Change in a Post 9/11 World*. New York: Palgrave.
Sanders, Arnie. "Critical Methods and the 20th-Century's 'Theory Wars.'" Goucher College. http://faculty.goucher.edu/eng215/Critical_Methods_and_20th_C_Theory_Wars.htm (accessed Aug. 9, 2012).
———. "English 215: Critical Methods (Spring 2013)." Goucher College. http://faculty.goucher.edu/eng215/ (accessed Feb. 14, 2013).
Saygin, A. P. 2011. "The Thing That Should Not Be: Predictive Coding and the Uncanny Valley in Perceiving Human and Humanoid Robot Actions." *Social Cognitive and Affective Neuroscience* 7: 413–422.
Scheff, T., and S. Retzinger. 1991. *Violence and Emotions*. Lexington, MA: Lexington Books.
Scheff, Thomas J. 2000. "Shame and the Social Bond: A Sociological Theory." *Sociological Theory* 18 (1): 84–99.
Sedgwick, E. 2003. *Touching Feeling: Affect, Pedagogy, Performativity*. Durham: Duke University Press.

Sedgwick, Eve, and Adam Frank, eds. 1995. *Shame and Its Sisters*. Durham: Duke University Press

Seidler, Guenter, and Frank E. Wagner. 2006. "Comparing the Efficacy of EMDR and Trauma-Focused Cognitive-Behavorial Therapy in the Treatment of PSD: A Meta-analytic Study." *Psychological Medicine* 36: 1515–1522. doi: http://dx.doi.org/10.1017/S0033291706007963.

Sharma, Ashok. 2013. "Hearings Trial Closed Indian Rape Case." *Washington Times*, Jan. 7. http://www.washingtontimes.com/news/2013/jan/7/hearings trial close Indian rape case/.

Sides, John, and Citrin, Jack. 2007. "How Large the Huddled Masses? The Causes and Consequences of Public Misperceptions about Immigrant Populations." Paper presented at the annual meeting of the Midwest Political Science Association, Lake Arrowhead, CA. http://scholar.google.com/citations?view_op=view_citation&hl=en&user=Y865yLYAAAAJ&citation_for_view=Y865yLYAAAAJ:WF5omc3nYNoC (accessed Aug. 20, 2012).

Siegel, Daniel. 1999. *The Developing Mind: How Relationships and the Brain Interact to Shape Who We Are*. New York: Guilford Press.

Siegel, Daniel J., Marion Solomon, and Diana Fosha. 2011. *The Healing Power of Emotion: Affective Neuroscience, Development & Clinical Practice*. New York: W. W. Norton.

Smith, Barbara Herrnstein. 1997. *Belief and Resistance*. Cambridge, MA: Harvard University Press.

Solms, Mark. 1995. "New Findings on the Neurological Organization of Dreaming: Implications for Psychoanalysis." *Psychoanalyic Quarterly* 64: 43–67.

———.1997. *The Neuropsychology of Dreams: A Clinico-Anatomical Study*. Mahwah, NJ: Lawrence Erlbaum.

Statement on Liberal Learning. 1998. Association of American Colleges and Universities. Adopted by the Board of Directors 1998. http://www.aacu.org/About/statements/liberal_learning.cfm (accessed July 3, 2012).

Stenning, Keith. 2002. *Seeing Reason: Image and Language in Learning to Think*. Cambridge: Oxford University Press.

Thomas, Beth. 2012. "Psychologizing and the Anti-Psychologist: Dewey and Contemporary Art Education." *Studies in Art Education: A Journal of Issues and Research* 53(4): 330–346.

Tomkins, Silvan S. 1962. *Affect, Imagery, Consciousness. Volume 1: The Positive Affects*. London: Tavistock.

———. 1963. *Affect, Imagery, Consciousness. Volume 2: The Negative Affects*. London: Tavistock.

Trainor, Jennifer Seibel. 2006. "From Identity to Emotion: Frameworks for Understanding, and Teaching against, Anticritical Sentiments in the Classroom." *JAC* 26 (3–4): 643–655.

Van der Kolk, Bessel. 1989. *Psychiatric Clinics of North America* 12: 389–411. http://www.cirp.org/library/psych/vanderkolk/.

———. 2005. "Developmental Trauma Disorder: A New, Rational Diagnosis for Children with Complex Trauma Histories." *Psychiatric Annals* 35: 401–404.

Volkan, Vamik. 1977. *Bloodlines.* Boulder, CO: West View Press.

———. 1988. *The Need to Have Enemies and Allies: From Clinical Practice to International Relationships.* Northvale, NJ: Jason Aronson Press.

Voltaire. (1764a) 1872. "Commentary." In *An Essay on Crimes and Punishments. By the Marquis Beccaria of Milan. With a Commentary by M. de Voltaire. A New Edition Corrected.* (Albany: W. C. Little). The Online Library of Liberty. http://oll.libertyfund.org/?option=com_staticxt&staticfile=show.php%3Ftitle=2193&chapter=202803&layout=html&Itemid=27 (accessed July 23, 2012).

———. (1764b) 1901. *The Works of Voltaire. A Contemporary Version.* A Critique and Biography by John Morley, notes by Tobias Smollett, translated by William F. Fleming. New York: E. R. DuMont. 21 vols. Vol. 6. *Philosophical Dictionary.* http://ebooks.adelaide.edu.au/v/voltaire/dictionary/chapter314.html (accessed Feb. 9, 2013).

Wasserman, M. D. 1984. "Psychoanalytic Dream Theory and Recent Neurobiological Findings about REM Sleep." *Journal of the American Psychoanalytic. Association* 32: 831–846.

Westen, Drew. 2007. *The Political Brain: The Role of Emotion in Deciding the Fate of the Nation.* New York: Public Affairs.

Wilson, E. O. 2012. *The Social Conquest of the Earth.* New York: Liveright Publishing Corporation.

Wilson, Timothy D. 2002. *Strangers to Ourselves: Discovering the Adaptive Unconscious.* Cambridge: Belknap Press.

Worsham, Lynn. 1998. "Going Postal: Pedagogic Violence and the Schooling of Emotion." *JAC: A Journal of Composition Theory* 18 (2): 213–245.

Zizek, Slavoj. 1992. *Enjoy Your Symptom.* New York: Routledge.

INDEX

Achebe, Chinua, 52–60
Alcorn, Marshall, 95
anger, 16, 29, 44, 46, 56, 60, 73, 89, 100, 115, 127, 130, 142, 151, 154, 174
anosognosia, 2–7, 10, 14, 17, 24, 29–30, 49, 63, 87, 101, 103, 140, 173
anxiety, 3, 28–34, 39–40, 44–6, 55–60, 65–7, 78, 90, 95, 99–101, 104, 106, 108, 110–11, 123, 127, 169, 176
Aristotle, 31, 46, 109
arousal, 45, 165
Association of American Colleges and Universities, 127

backfire effect, 22, 107
Bain, Ken, 7, 9, 11, 36–7, 56
belief, 1–4, 9–13, 18–22, 29, 34–5, 43–8, 68–71, 78, 83–90, 93–111, 129–50, 165–6, 177
Berman, Jeffrey, 117–19, 129
Bion, Wilfried, 11, 28–33, 39, 48–52, 56–66, 77–8, 109, 119, 121, 141, 165
  attack on linking, 48, 64, 77, 82, 125, 150
  −K, 11, 48–50, 58–60, 64
  K, L and H, 48–50, 62–4
Biran, Adam, 183
Bisiach, E., M., 27
Bracher, Mark, 41, 170

brain, 2–48, 83, 97, 101, 103, 108, 135, 140–1, 150, 153, 156–8, 163–7, 170–6
Brooks, David, 14
Brothers, Doris, 175
Bryson, Bill, 7–8
Burgess, H., 59–60
Burke, Kenneth, 141–2

Cartwright, R. D., 27, 28
Caruth, Cathy, 136–8, 142, 149
Charles, Marilyn, 167
childhood trauma, 172–3, 176
chosen trauma, 168
Critin, Jack, 106
Clark-Ibanez, Marisol, 160–2
Conrad, Joseph, 52–5, 58–61, 98, 103
Cozolino, Louis, 103
Cronon, William, 146
Curtis, V., 83

Damasio, Antonio, 13–17, 24–30, 44–9, 65, 79, 144
Davis, Katherine, 112
defense, 18, 40, 58–60, 95, 99, 106, 149, 146, 168
democracy, 5, 47, 69, 71, 93–4, 126
denial, 22, 25, 40
desire not to know, 22, 28–34, 38–9, 47, 52–60, 67, 76, 79, 82, 86–90
developmental trauma disorder, 173

Dewey, John, 126
disbelief, 12, 20–1, 140
disgust, 44, 54, 77–86, 174
dissociation, 150, 154, 174–5, 177
Dodge, Kenneth, 32
Douglas, Frederick, 166
dream, 10–13, 19, 27–8, 35–7, 68, 175

Eagleton, Terry, 47
Ekman, Paul, 83
Elsaesser, Thomas, 159
EMDR, 27
emotion, 17–19, 31–8, 40–1, 49–60, 68–79, 86–96, 106–20, 125–34, 160–5
emotional assimilation, 13, 19–20, 23–8, 34, 40, 46, 75, 88, 91, 155, 160, 164, 166
emotional attachment, 115–17
emotional growth, 126–8
emotional resistance, 95
emotional work, 39, 75, 95, 128
evidence, 1–6, 19–22, 101–10

facial expression, 83, 161
facts, 23, 94, 160
Farrell, J. G., 31–2, 49–50, 129
fear, 3, 24, 28–32, 40, 44–6, 49, 64, 101, 108, 111–19, 128–9, 139, 145, 149–50, 169
feeling
  adjusting of, 18, 51
  conflicting, 34, 46, 73, 115
  and emotion, 17, 44, 63
  revision of, 35
  and thought, 83, 127
  and words, 71
Felman, Shoshona, 40
Filene, Peter, 112
Fish, Stanley, 1–4, 10, 20, 29, 46, 102, 141
Foulkes, David, 28
Frank, Arthur, 79, 128

Freud, Sigmund, 11, 18–19, 22, 68, 82, 94–5, 99, 102–3, 174–6

Gage, Amity, ix–x
gaps, ix–x
Garfinkel, Sarah N., 171
Garske, John, 112
Giroux, Henry A, 40
global integration, 156–60
Goleman, Daniel, 6
Greenway, H. D. S., 170
grief, 96, 103

Hagener, Malte, 159
Hale, Sharon Joy Ng, 162
Halloun, Inbrahim About, 6, 12
Hardy, Thomas, 158–60, 176
Harpham, Geoffrey, 44–5, 163–4
Herman, Judith, 96
Hestenes, David, 6, 12
holocaust denial, 1, 4
Holodynski, Manfred, 177
humanities, 55–6, 59, 126, 130, 144, 163, 167

identification, 118
illness, 128
image, 14–17, 28, 53, 82
information
  as needing emotional work for assimilation, 40, 91
  as stored in memory and not utilized, 28
  as uncomfortable experience, 22, 30
  as work of the university, 37–8

Jacobs, Dale, 41
Jerit, Jennifer, 106–7

Kafka, Alexander, 35, 37
Kandel, Eric, 37
Kelly, Vernon, 82

Keohane, Joe, 21–2
Klein, Melanie, 82
Kline, Peter, 12
knowing
  as emotional work, 48, 128
  as integration of emotion, 28, 128
  as loss, 128
Kort, B., 161–2
Kronast, Stefanie, 177
Kuklinski, James, 106–7

Lacan, Jacques, 40–52, 60, 133
Lakshmi, Rama, 156
language, 15–16, 99, 111, 121, 123, 130, 138–40
LeDoux, Josep., 12–13, 23, 45
Lenzi, J., 62–3
liberal education, 34–6, 38, 127, 146, 160, 178
Liberty Zone Café, 69–73, 86–7
Liberzon, Israel, 171

Mailer, Norman, 113–15, 129
Martin, Daniel, 112
Marx, Karl, 40, 66–77, 86–90
Masse, Michelle, x
Matthiessen, P, 85–6
Meltzer, Donald, 141
memory, 9–13, 23–49, 62, 75–6, 89, 95–6, 102–3, 138, 169, 170–5
Micciche, Laura, 41
Michels, Spencer, 160
mind, 2–18, 20, 28–30, 37, 60, 77, 107, 126–7, 163
mourning, 95–6

Nadel, Lynn, 28
narrative, 28, 53–4, 58, 77, 91, 96, 113, 128, 145, 159, 163, 166
neuroaesthetics, 35–7
neuroscience, 13, 24, 35, 38, 41, 103

Nussbaum, Martha, 34
Nyhan, Brendan, 98, 107

Olson, Gary, 102
online teaching, 37–8, 155, 160–4

paranoia, 93
passion for ignorance, 40–1, 62, 94, 139, 143, 177
Patterson, Stephen, 65
Payne, Jessica D., 28
pedagogy, 40, 65, 90
Perkins, Charlotte Gilman, 32, 129
Perry, B. D, 171, 175
Picard, R. W., 161–2
political behavior, 21, 95, 107, 169
Porter, Katherine Anne, 30
power, 75
pride, 24, 39, 44, 84, 91, 151, 169
psychosis, 96–7, 102

Quirk, Paul J., 106–7

Ramachandran, V. S., 2–35, 63, 87, 96, 103, 140–1, 173–4
rape, 117–19, 129, 156–60, 167–70
rationality, 3, 16, 20, 24, 32, 56, 94, 135
Ray, Oakley, 128
reflection, 15, 33, 35–6
Reifler, Jason, 98, 107
Reilly, R., 161–2
REM, 10–11, 35
resistance, 10, 23, 40–1, 48, 56–7, 65–6, 72, 75–83, 86, 90, 95, 95, 98, 101, 106–8
Retzinger, S., 85
reverie, 37, 151
Revonsuo, Antti, 28
Rich, Robert, 106–7

Rokeach, Milton, 96–11
Russell, Bertrand, 128

Samuels, Robert, 41
Sanders, Arnie, 130–2
Saunders, Bernard, 12
Saygin, A. P, 19
Scheff, T., 77, 85
Schwieder, David, 106–7
Scott, Linda, 160–2
Sedgwick, E., 77–9
Seidler, Guenter, 27
shame, 24, 29, 39, 40, 44, 67, 77–91
Sharma, Ashok, 158
Sides, John, 106
Siegel, Daniel, 27–8, 39, 45
silence, 36–7, 53, 64, 66, 73, 79, 89–90, 125, 128, 130
Smith, Barbara Herrnstein, 22
social bond, 68, 79, 79, 89, 112–13, 118
Solms, Mark, 28
Sorenson, E. R., 83
Stenning, Keith, 9, 23–4
suffering, 90, 159, 166–7
symptom, 103
symptomatic fixation, 95, 104

theory wars, 125, 130–3
therapeutic Alliance, 112
therapy, 38, 44, 112
Thomas, Beth, 35
thought
  as defensive, 15, 21, 30, 45
  defined by Bion, 60–6, 165
  defined by Damasio, 17
  described by Stanley Fish, 1–2
  as determined by emotional undertones, 63
  as determined by traumatic experience, 165, 168–77
  emotion as generative ground of, 39
  as generated by social bonds, 111, 129
  as ideoaffective structure, 102
  as links in representation, 3, 27–32, 39, 44, 58, 64–8, 77, 82, 175
  as needing emotional integration, 30
  as symptomatic, 102–11
Tomkins, Silvan S., 77–82, 85–9
Trainor, Jennifer Seibel, 91
trauma, 27, 96, 102–8, 135–57, 168–78

uncanny, 19–20
unconscious, 10–22, 39, 45, 48, 59, 62, 79, 82, 88, 118, 161, 167–9, 177
unconscious knowledge, 14, 39, 48, 82, 177

Van der Kolk, Bessel, 172–5
violence, 63–4, 102–4, 110, 135, 155–6, 172–3
Volkan, Vamik, 168–71
Voltaire, 97

Wagner, Frank E., 27
Wallace, Friesen, 83
Westen, Drew, 22
Wilson, E. O., 134–5
Wilson, Timothy D., 18
Worsham, Lynn, 1, 41, 102

Zizek, Slavoj, 177

GPSR Compliance

The European Union's (EU) General Product Safety Regulation (GPSR) is a set of rules that requires consumer products to be safe and our obligations to ensure this.

If you have any concerns about our products, you can contact us on

ProductSafety@springernature.com

In case Publisher is established outside the EU, the EU authorized representative is:

Springer Nature Customer Service Center GmbH
Europaplatz 3
69115 Heidelberg, Germany

www.ingramcontent.com/pod-product-compliance
Lightning Source LLC
LaVergne TN
LVHW012101070526
838200LV00074BA/3889